Dear Latoya

Experiencing

the 25th

hour

TRANSFORMING YOUR PAIN INTO POSSIBILITIES

Be abundantly

Advantage
INSPIRATIONAL

Psalm 27

BEVERLY MORRISON CAESAR

Experiencing The 25ᵗʰ Hour by Beverly Morrison Caesar
Copyright © 2005 Beverly Morrison Caesar
All Rights Reserved
ISBN: 1-59755-026-4

Published by: *ADVANTAGE BOOKS*™
 www.advbooks.com

Unless otherwise indicated, Bible quotations are taken from the
King James Version of the Bible. Copyright ©1984, by Thomas
Nelson.

Some of the names in this book were changed.

Visit us at **www.the25thhour.biz**

Library of Congress Control Number: 2005928473

First Printing: July 2005

07 08 09 10 11 12   9 8 7 6 5 4 3 2 1

Printed in the United States of America

Dedication

This memoir is dedicated to my parents, **Hector and Veronica Morrison** who heeded the voice of God in their 25th hour, to grant me life.

I also dedicate this book to my only son, **Roderick Richardson Caesar lll,** a miracle sent from God for a divinely destined purpose.

I also devote this memoir to the memory of all the aborted fetuses that did not have a chance at life.

And, finally, this dedication goes to the preemies who are struggling to make it outside the security of their mother's womb -- struggling to survive at the hands of science and machine.

Beverly Morrison Caesar

Endorsements

When I read this book, ***Experiencing The 25th Hour,*** little did I know that I was going on a journey to realms unknown and also very familiar paths. Being Beverly's only brother and separated by distance, a lot of life's issues are passed without note. However, her book has brought me up to date on the challenges that life offered her. Reading this book was extremely interesting as she sought to show how the Almighty God, the Everlasting Father, and the Prince of Peace is deeply involved in our lives - leading, preventing, healing, giving and taking. What is clearly seen from reading this book is how The Ancient of Days prevented an abortion, then as Present Help in time of trouble - He caused the miracle of birth, and now He continues to reign as the Everlasting Father.

Elder Dennis A. Morrison,
Marverly Gospel Hall, Jamaica, W. I.

"For the eyes of the Lord search back and forth across the whole earth, looking for people whose hearts are perfect toward him, so that He can show His great power in helping them." 2Corinthians 16:9 (L.B.) ***Experiencing The 25th Hour*** is a compelling and riveting chronicle to the power, truth and personal witness of the reality of this verse. In it, my good friend, Beverly, beautifully testifies of the miracles, which have blessed the world with two lives: which without Christ's direct intervention, would not have existed. I thank God for the gift of Beverly Caesar's life to the world; for her love of life and devotion to Christ, her family, her friends and all God's children. Only eternity will reveal the multitude who will spend time without end in heaven because of these two specific miracles which resulted in the lives of Beverly Caesar and her son, Roderick Caesar, III.

Janet Broling, Women's Prayer Summit, NYC

Experiencing The 25th Hour speaks into the lives of individuals as they make the hard choices that life presents. It helps to know that we are not alone, as Satan would like us to believe, as we seek to lead a victorious Christian life. Pastor Beverly Morrison Caesar's story provides hope and encouragement to the reader. It is a powerful testimony of God's goodness, the power of prayer and the importance of faith.

Dr. Bishop Ernestine C. Reems
Center of Hope Community Church, Oakland, CA

As a childhood friend of Beverly, I have personally witnessed God's call on her life, her humanness and, in the final analysis, her obedience to His Word. This book beautifully details life challenges, difficult choices and the resolve to stay the course, not only for Beverly but also for the entire Caesar family. We can learn valuable life lessons of unconditional love, faith and courage as we read this book.

Sharon Wood-Dunn, President
S. Wood Wilson Associates

This is a book that reflects the open and honest heart of the author. Beverly has learned the meaning of walking with God in public and private blessings as well as deep trials. As you enter her journey into the lessons she learned about walking by faith in all circumstances of life, you will discover the footprints of God's presence are always with His children.

Vonette Z. Bright, Co-Founder
Campus Crusade For Christ, International

This is a story that will hold the reader in its grip for weeks and months. An honest portrayal of a woman's struggle in holding on to God's promises while the life of her son hangs in the balance! Her determination to follow the dream and the God given mission to her family and to her church lets us see Christian principles in action. We owe Beverly Caesar thanks for keeping a stirring journal of her rich and colorful life, one filled with the depth that comes from living with God continually.

Dr. Friedhelm K. Radandt
President Emeritus, The Kings College, NYC

This book is more than just a memoir. It is an empowering, equipping, and endowing book that will challenge you to turn your trials into triumphant victories. As you walk with Beverly through her personal journey of faith, you will sense that she is holding your hands as she leads you down familiar paths. You will be furnished with the tools necessary to make right choices as you are guided to a place of fulfillment.

The Hon. Rev. Floyd H. Flake, D.Min.
Pastor of The Greater Allen A.M.E. Cathedral of New York
U. S. Congressman, Retired

Beverly Morrison Caesar

About The Author

Beverly Morrison Caesar is the wife of Dr. Bishop Roderick R. Caesar, Senior Pastor of Bethel Gospel Tabernacle, in Queens, New York. **Pastor Bev,** as she is affectionately called**,** is an ordained minister and serves along side her husband in pastoring this historical church.

A busy mother of four, she adjusts her schedule to home school her two younger children, ages 16 and 12; oversees the women's ministry of Bethel; is the editor- in -chief of the church's publication department; conducts the Speech Choir, and is the director of the A. C. T. Ministry- *Arts in Christian Theater*. **Beverly** is a dramatist and a playwright. She has written, directed and produced several successful plays that benefited the Queens community.

Pastor Bev served on the Executive Committee of the Women's Prayer Summit, a tri-state prayer ministry for women and to women. This ministry conducted two women's prayer meetings at the Theater at Madison Square Garden, NY, with over 6, 000 women from all denominations and ethnicity praying as one.

She obtained her bachelors of Science and bachelors of Theology degrees from Hunter College and the Bethel Bible Institute, respectively. She devotes her time to the Lord, to her husband and family, and to the ministries to which she has been called.

Beverly is a workshop teacher, seminar conductor and expositor of God's word.

Pastor Bev resides in Queens with her husband of 26 years, and their three daughters Naomi, Lydia, Elizabeth and their miracle son, Roderick III. She is the proud grandmother of an 18 - month - old baby girl, Kayliah.

Acknowledgements

Completing this memoir was a combined effort of several individuals who played a key role in this task. I thank my husband, Roderick, for his unwavering support. His encouragement gave me the impetus to complete the project. My children, Naomi, Lydia, Roderick III and Elizabeth, never complained when they "lost" me for days on end as I worked on the memoir. I know that the best children in the world reside on Hollis Avenue, in Queens, New York.

Support from my extended family encouraged me to stay the course and remain focused. Thanks go to Beverly Caesar-Sherrod, Rhonda Coy, Robyn Edwards, Dennis and Benita Morrison and my mom, Veronica Morrison.

Recognition is extended to Gwendolyn Sharpe, Gina Gratia-Carr, Crystal Joseph, Linda Smith, Janet Broling, Sharon Wood-Dunn and Jacqueline McCullough who offered godly support that pushed me to excel.

Thanks to the many women of Bethel Gospel Tabernacle who gave me that extra "nudge" to pen this memoir.

Special gratitude goes to the editors and proofreaders who worked around the clock to make this an excellent representation of our Lord. Dawn Armand, Naomi Caesar, Beverly Delgado, Elaine Lee, Stephen Samuel, Karlene Jackson-Thompson, Andrea Turner, Michael Torres and Marcia Williams.

Thanks to the office staff for their assistance in making this project a reality. Colin Morris, Leota Figgins and Charles Washington offered critical and crucial help in the management of this memoir, thank you!

"Hats off"to Karlene Jackson-Thompson for her sensitivity, creativity and her relentless dedication to this project. Naomi's hard work and thoroughness propelled this project into what I conceive as greatness.

Recognition goes to Advantage Books and the qualified staff who steered this project in the right direction. You helped make a dream come true. May the blessings of the Lord overtake you, is my prayer.

May the Lord abundantly bless each of you for the gift of your talent and the sacrifice of your time to me and to the cause of Christ.

Foreword

Driving down the Brooklyn Queens Expressway, I saw a billboard advertisement, paraphrased, stated that, *"pain was weakness being released."* I believe that **Experiencing The 25th Hour** will afford you the insight on how to transfer your pain, powerlessness, hopelessness and faithlessness into an awareness of your unfathomable strength, possibilities and opportunities.

In many of our theologies, we are trapped with the notion that pain, suffering, and disappointments should be subverted, suppressed, and stifled. It is the turning of sorrow into joy; midnight into day; wrong into right; shame into honor; and defeat into victory that makes the Christian experience truly a reflection of Christ's power and authority.

Walk through this book, hear the writer's story and then discern your story of victory, which comes through your relationship with Jesus Christ. He is the one, who takes what was intended for evil and uses it for your good.

Pastor Jacqueline E. McCullough
Beth Rapha House of Healing

Table of Contents

Introduction

I propose a question to you for consideration. Have you ever aborted a divine plan God had for your life because of a choice you made? I am sure your answer will be somewhat affirmative. This memoir not only deals with physical abortion, but with spiritual and emotional abortion. Attempts to circumvent the plans God has for your life and for the life of your family and for the life of your church. Come walk with me as we journey through the life-altering events that unfolded in my life to bring me to a place of fullness.

A journey where God showed up.

A journey where God proved His omnipotence.

A journey where God delivered His promise.

When it seemed as if all was lost, as if the hands of time had served its fatal blow, God stepped in!

Come and experience with me the hand of God in an hour that belongs only to Him

- - The 25th hour.

As you read what God revealed to me, I hope you will find within these pages that the divine plan of God upon a life is greater than the devourer's attempt to terminate those plans - - a life determined to please God at any cost despite human frailties and detours. The lyrics to one of Rev. Donnie McClurkin's songs encourage us to 'get up', if we made a mistake, and to try again. He sings, "We fall down but we get up; for a saint is just a sinner who fell down and got up." This song speaks of the wondrous miracle of God's grace - - His grace cannot be bought by fame, fortune or reputation - - an undeserved benefit!

In detailing some of my experiences, I hope that you will find yourself in this memoir or relate to something written within these pages. I am sure that your faith in God will increase as you read how the Almighty Creator unfolded His plans to bring my family and me into the fullness of His grace, mercy and glory. As I communicate with emotional honesty, I hope that you will hear what the Lord is saying to you. God's wonder will expand before your very eyes, as you walk with me through the many miracles that have graced my life. I hope you will become keenly aware that your life is a miracle and that everything that takes place in it is under the full scrutiny of the Lord. I also pray that you will become acutely cognizant of your God-given gifts, recognizing that your life is not an accident.

It is my intent, by the grace of God, that as you read each chapter your faith will increase and you will embrace your predestined assignment.

Physical abortion is devastating, but so are the spiritual and emotional abortions that plague many people today. Satan has unleashed his strategies upon the earth, and if we remain asleep, we will end up aborting the wonderful miracles God has for us. Unfortunately, physical abortion is irrevocable - - only eternity will reveal the effects. However, as God's children, we have the ability to reverse the emotional and spiritual abortions that once plagued us and breathe life back into our existence and begin to live again for the glory of God.

Chapter One

THE PLAN

Hand in hand they walked up the hill to the doctor's office. Veronica, affectionately called Mae, was fully engrossed in thought as she contemplated the decision she was about to make. Questions flooded her already over-taxed mind. *Is this the best choice? What if I die during the procedure? Will it be painful? What about God? Certainly He understands my dilemma!* She could not control the bombardment of questions that enveloped her every thought. She looked at Hector, and wondered what was going on in his mind. As if he read her thoughts, he blurted out, "It's going to be okay, you'll see. You have nothing to worry about. Don't forget, Hyacinth did the same thing, and look at her now, going on with her life and worry free." Somehow those words were not assuring to Mae. Yes, she was worried! Yes, she was unsure if this was the right thing to do. *I was too young and immature to even understand what happened with Hyacinth behind those closed doors. Sure, she did it, but should I do it?* She could not eliminate the thoughts and the questions.

Mae Tafft Morrison was born and raised in Jamaica, W. I. It was instilled in her from a child that attending mass was crucial to one's spiritual growth; therefore she attended mass faithfully and regularly. She knew that God was interested in her. As she reflected on her first pregnancy, she remembered her prayer to God, *"If you give me a male child, I will give him back to you. I want him to grow up to be a man of God."* When her son, Dennis, was born, she knew God had definitely heard her prayers. Immediately he was baptized, and Mae kept in her heart the promise she had made to God.

Less than 18 months later she gave birth to a sickly, asthmatic baby girl who kept them extremely occupied and broke. The cramped, cold apartment added to the dilemma. Hector's carpentry business was not doing well, and Mae could not go back to work - - not yet. His mother would not help. Furthermore, she regularly sneered at Mae for taking her son away from her. She even tried to sabotage their wedding. She vowed that she would have nothing to do with them, ever! For many years it was Mae who struggled to maintain an amicable relationship among all three of them. Who were they to turn to? Her mother, "Mammy," as she was tenderly called, lived in the country - - too far for consistent help. The doctor's bills were pouring in. Hector's carpentry business was not bringing in enough income for the family to meet their financial obligations with any level of consistency; their indebtedness increased and added to the already mounting challenges, an unexpected crisis emerged!

Hector, in his zeal to make ends meet for his growing family, made an unwise decision. One windy, rainy day, he received a visit from Mr. James McPherson, a wealthy Jamaican businessman who traveled extensively to America and Europe. This man could very well have imported any furniture he wanted. He knew that the skill and craftsmanship of Hector were unmatched; therefore he secured Hector's business. Additionally, Hector had access to his father-in law's farm from which he could acquire some Cedar trees to build what Mr. McPherson requested. Money and promise were exchanged and each man went back to his own home, one to the warmth and comfort of a large dwelling, the other to a cold, small and damp place with two small toddlers. Figuring that he had time on his hands, and knowing that he was capable of fulfilling the request, Hector spent the money on his family's needs.

One month later, Mr. McPherson called on Hector for his armoire to find out that not only was the chest not complete, but his money had obviously been spent elsewhere.

"I want my money or my chest," yelled Mr. McPherson.

"Give me some more time, and you'll get the chest" begged Hector.

"You've had your time and my money," came the response. "I'm not here to negotiate or bargain with you. All I want is the chest or the money."

"You'll get the chest. I promise. Just a few more days, please," implored Hector. "This is not how I operate, but money was tight. The baby stays sick, and I needed to buy medicine for her and food for the family. Business is slower than I expected, but I promise, I'll get the chest to you next week."

"A promise is a comfort to a fool, and I don't care about your dilemma. I'm no fool. Just give me what I paid for and I'll leave you alone, but I'm not leaving until you produce either the chest or my cash!" Hector got down on his hands and knees pleading for mercy. The police were called; Hector got arrested and spent one month in jail for his indiscretion. From this experience, he realized that they would be better off if the family moved to the country with Mae's mother.

Living in Jamaica, West Indies afforded them the opportunity of surviving off the fruitfulness of the rich and healthy soil of the country. Hector and Mae left the city and moved into the rural town of Palm, St. Catherine, to raise their two children, Dennis and Sandra. Palm, as its name implies, was graced with palm trees, and coconut trees that lined the lush and green countryside for miles on end. Certainly the air would be better for Sandra, and the closeness to Grandma would help. No one could conjure up a more natural, healthier medicine than Mammy. She knew just what little Sandra needed to make her well. The shaded front yard with orange and grapefruit trees was a welcome relief from a stressful city life. Vegetable patches, banana trees, sugar cane plants, graced the backyard and a variety of tealeaves grew near the brook. Mae could relax a little and eventually find a job close by and go on with her life, so she thought.

"Pregnant, again?! We can barely make it with these two, much less another! Sandra needs a lot of attention, and Dennis is getting into everything!" Mae understood Hector's outburst, but she did not expect his next statement. "You have to get rid of it. We can't have another baby, not now. It is too costly to have all these children. I'll kill myself trying to keep this family together." Her mind was wandering as he spoke, agreeing with every word he uttered, except the 'getting rid of it' part.

"Are you listening to me, Mae?"

"Of course I am," was her faint reply.

"Well, what do you have to say?"

"I don't know. My mind is spinning. My thoughts are unclear. I cannot seem to focus on what is happening. So much . . . so quickly."

"If we do it now it won't seem like such a big deal, because it is not even really a 'baby' yet. Mae, please understand that I am not trying to be pushy or insensitive, but I know we cannot have this baby . . . we are unable to take care of three small children so close in age."

"I know, I know, it's just that. . ." her words trailed off.

"Talk to cousin Hyacinth. She did it, and look at her now. She's all right. Remember, you were there with her almost through the whole process? The sooner we get this over with the better, and I promise you that later on when we become more stable, we can have more children, I promise." His plea was imploring. It sounded a little more palatable. Hector was right. They could hardly make it without 'Mammy. ' Sandra demanded a lot of attention, and Dennis, not yet toilet trained, was quite a handful. The children needed her undivided attention, and another baby would definitely be too much for them to handle. God would understand, and when things got better, they'd have more children. Well, it was settled in her mind.

Mae began to recapitulate the circumstances under which Hyacinth, who was blind from birth, got her abortion. How could she ever forget being there with Hyacinth, holding her hands and encouraging her every step of the way? As a young girl, Mae, was not fully aware of what was about to happen to Hyacinth. She remembered the embarrassment Hyacinth expressed, knowing that the baby was illegitimate. They were both worried for the baby, because Alton, the father, was also blind and they wondered if the child would be born blind. The option seemed plausible and conclusive.

For a blind woman, Hyacinth was fiercely independent and strong-willed. She lived alone, cooked, washed and cleaned all by herself. Mae was there for moral support. When the day came for the procedure, Mae walked with her to the hospital. The doctor allowed Mae to accompany Hyacinth, but only up to a certain point. The procedure was quick, and the next day, Hyacinth was home. Mae often wondered what happened behind those closed doors. Approximately one year after the abortion, Hyacinth and Alton married and they seemed happy together. It was time to pay Hyacinth a visit.

The next morning, Mae walked to Hyacinth's and found her in the yard hanging up the wash. Little fourteen month-old, Joshua, thumb in mouth, was hanging onto the safety of his mom's skirt. Mae picked him up; he was puny and small for his age and very much sighted. She inquired about how Hyacinth was doing and began helping her with the wash.

"I'm doing...just doing," was Hyacinth's hasty reply. "What's up with you?"

"Well, Hyacinth, I'm pregnant again," said Mae with dejection. "I am thinking about getting rid of it. I really don't want to, but Hector is encouraging me."

"Well, that's your business," came the quick reply.

"Please don't tell anyone. I would be embarrassed if they knew I was pregnant again, and more embarrassed if they found out I got rid of it."

"Mae, you have to live your life for yourself. Nobody knows what you are going through when you go home to a house full of kids and not enough food to feed them all."

"I know what you mean."

"Can you imagine if I had kept the first one? I would have had a toddler running around the yard, and Joshua, barely able to walk, clinging to my leg. Oh no! I'm glad I did it."

"You seem to be doing okay. Is everything all right?"

"Well, like I say, this is my life. Nobody has to know my business and I keep it that way. People talk too much, and they don't know what's going on behind closed doors. I make sure my husband eats, and that Joshua has enough to eat. I keep mostly to myself. Marcia is the only person I talk to, you know, just in case something happens to me. So I do not owe anyone any explanation. Let them talk. I know what's happening in my house. So go to the doctor and get your abortion. I'm glad I did, and so will you." Hyacinth made a lot of sense. She talked with persuasion, and Mae was convinced. They chatted for a few more minutes, and then, Mae thanked her and left feeling quite sure that this was the best course of action to take. However, there was still a lingering, haunting, uncertain feeling about the whole thing.

One week later, after much discussion, Hector and Mae took the long, tedious walk to the clinic. They arrived at the building, which was located at the top of a steep hill. A white, bright building with well manicured grounds, and a high wrought iron gate announced the front of the building. Mae's heart pounded, as they got closer to the gate. *Why do I feel so nervous?* She asked herself. No reply. *Hector seems so composed, so self-assured. Isn't he worried, or even a little nervous? Why should he worry?* Came her own mind's response, *He's not having the procedure done, you are!* She whispered a quick prayer, *God protect me in this. One day I will see my baby in heaven. The Virgin Mary will keep her safe, as you will keep me safe, Amen.*

By the time they reached the gate, they were both exhausted from the long trek. A tall, slender, distinguished gentleman was about to lift the latch on the gate to open it, when he asked if they needed assistance. He appeared to be in deep thought. Hector took the plunge, stated their purpose with clarity, and paused. To their amazement, the gentleman indicated that he indeed was the doctor. He took one look at Mae, turned to face her, and stepped back. With a startled, puzzled, look he began to rub his eyes. His eyes never left her face. He shook his head as if to say, "No." He looked her up and down, perplexed, shaking and stuttering, "I cannot touch you!" He sputtered out; "I. . . I. . . I. . . have never seen anything like this before. There is a. . . a. . . a. . . a glow. A light around you. . . something is around you, almost like an angel. Bu. . . . t it can't be. I can't touch you. No one can touch you. You must have this baby. You are protected and no one can touch you." His piercing, sharp eyes never left Mae's bewildered face. He slowly stepped back, wished them well and disappeared into the clinic.

Hector and Mae stood as if transfixed for what seemed to be hours. He looked at her and she looked at him. "What was that all about? Why did he leave us out here without telling us more? What angel? What light? What glow? We saw nothing! What do we do now?" Here came the questions again, this time they were questions of life. Mae's mind was in a whirlwind. The whirlwind began to clear up and she felt the presence of God warm her heart.

"Hector, do you know what this means? We have to have this baby! He said no one should touch me. Did you see his face? He looked frightened, but he was calm and he spoke clearly. Did you see his eyes? I don't understand what just happened, but this I do know, I feel happy and peaceful about keeping this child. God visited us Hector. God stopped what we were about to do because something will be different about this child! God prevented the abortion!"

"Mae, if I did not see this for myself, I would not have believed you. You are right. We must have this baby." They left the clinic, walking assuredly with each step; knowing that if God could speak to a doctor in such an unusual way, then He must be able to take care of three little children. Seven months later, a chubby daughter, weighing ten pounds was born to Hector and Mae Morrison in the comfort of their humble home. When the midwife arrived and she saw the beautiful bundle, she smiled and said, "We should dress her up in a pink dress and show her off." They named her Beverly.

The plan was to destroy a life, a life destined by God. The plan came from the deceiver of the brethren, none other than Lucifer. But God supernaturally intervened through the voice of a non-believer to circumvent the design of the enemy. God uses whomever He chooses to fulfill His divine purpose in the lives of those He loves. He saw Veronica's heart, knew that it was tender toward Him, and honored her. He kept his pulse on Hector, the man with the solution, and showed him who was in control. He strategically placed a doctor at the opportune time to see an angel, receive the message and deliver it accurately. This doctor was not to deliver death, but life instead to this family. The psalmist declares in Psalm 127 verse 3, "Lo, children are an heritage of the Lord, and the fruit of the womb is His reward." God is the giver of life. He blesses families as it pleases Him. But Satan was not finished. His intent was to snuff out this life before birth, and if he was not successful then, he had to go another route. He had other tactics up his sleeves.

During their stay at Mammy's, Hector and Mae experienced another close call. It happened one evening when Beverly was about three months old and peacefully asleep in the only bed (full size) they owned. You see, when they moved in with Mammy, there was no place to put the crib but on top of a wardrobe, made at the skilled hands of Hector. Hector also made the crib using solid cedar wood. The crib weighed about 50 pounds and was quite awkward to maneuver. He placed it securely on top of the six-foot mahogany wardrobe so that only a major earthquake could jolt it out of its position. No one could reach the crib but him. He made sure of that.

On that evening, as was customary, little Hubert, a neighbor's five-year old son, was visiting. He enjoyed looking at Beverly and playing with her pink cheeks. Suddenly, out of nowhere, came a scream from Hubert as he ran out of the house yelling, "She's dead, the baby is dead! Come quick!" Mae ran into the house to find the crib on top of the infant - - or so she thought. She ran out of the house, holding her head and screaming, "My baby, my baby, the crib killed her, the crib killed my baby." Mammy rushed in, wiped her hands on her apron and investigated the situation. Not only was the crib on the bed, but it was also less than one inch from the child's head! From the doorway, all anyone could see was the crib and no baby! A full size bed with a baby asleep in the middle of it made a sure target for a falling crib.

Mammy faced the situation and went into the room only to find Beverly fast asleep. Mammy was awe - struck at the miracle, for indeed it was a miracle. For all practical purposes, the crib should have killed the child from the manner in which it toppled from the wardrobe; it should have landed on top of the child, but another angel intervened and spared the life of Beverly. Again, Satan's attempt was aborted. Only a slight scrape grazed her forehead. Not enough to awaken a sleeping, protected, and contented infant. In Psalm 34:7, we read, "The angel of the Lord encampeth round about them that fear Him, and delivereth them." A God-fearing grandmother and a young mother, who recently experienced conversion through her new birth in Jesus, gave thanks to God for His supernatural, divine protection. The Lord showed up at the 25th hour to ensure the safety of His child.

Life continued to progress for the Morrisons. After Beverly, Mae lost two infants at child - birth, and Maxine was born almost five years later. They successfully evolved from under the pressures of life to finally own their own home in Kingston. It was small, but it was home! Hector landed a job at the Kingston Penitentiary where he worked his way up to the position of warden. Mae worked at the nearby Colgate factory.

It was in this home, when at the age of twelve, another experience almost took Beverly's "breath" away. In the process of unscrewing a lighted bulb to transfer it to another lamp, she used a scarf to hold the hot bulb. Unfortunately, the scarf got caught in the bulb's socket causing electrical shock waves to transfer into Beverly, catapulting her across the room with force that literally took her breath away. She recalls thinking that she was going to die; "I remember feeling as if the breath was being sucked out of my lungs. I was choking! I knew I was going to die. It was an awful frightening feeling, one I will never forget!" She was left almost lifeless in the arms of Mae, violently shaking and trembling.

Miraculously, the electric shock left no marks of physical injury - - nothing, that time could not heal. However, Beverly became emotionally paralyzed, afraid to go back into the room where the incident took place. She became phlegmatic, forgetful and listless. She was afraid to sleep alone, and had to have the lights on. She became jumpy and nervous about everything. Her attention in school faltered; fear controlled her every move. At the sight of any lamp, the fear of death overwhelmed her. Death became a common thought of hers. Her screams at night awoke everyone in the house. Her nightmares became regular occurrences.

At her grandmother's house in Linstead, every fear intensified. Living in the country, where street - lights were limited; Beverly became increasingly afraid of the dark. She would not dare venture outside alone at nights. Any errands that had to be done after dark were given to her sisters. She also began to lose weight due to a loss of appetite. At that time, no one attributed the electrical incident to her sudden change in behavior; until a doctor's visit indicated that perhaps something traumatic had taken place in her life. Her grandmother's concern intensified, and she did everything within her power to get to the root of Beverly's change in disposition. As Beverly began to painfully recall the incident, and with the help of her family, she was able to rid herself of the fear of dying, so that her life could get back to normalcy. It was a painful process for Beverly. Whenever she had to recall the event she would begin to shake uncontrollably. She stuttered when speaking, her face became ashen and the blood disappeared from her cheeks. She showed signs of being visibly shaken. Her grandmother prayed for her. She had the believers at Linstead Gospel Hall call out Beverly's name before the Lord. Slowly and gradually Beverly pressed on. This took some time, but thanks to God, the experience slowly became history. She was able to fight off the anxiety attacks, to ward off the fear of death, and she was able to come through victoriously. Because of the love of her family and the prayers of God's people she prevailed. Satan wanted to take her mind at the tender age of twelve, but again God intervened. She became engrossed in Sunday school, memorizing the scriptures and singing praises unto the Lord. God's Word became her source of strength.

The sovereign God had plans for me, Beverly, and He kept the devourer away, in order to fulfill His sacred design for my life. Jeremiah 29:11 has served to encourage and confirm to me that I serve a God who is indeed mindful of me; "For I know the thoughts that I think toward you, saith the Lord, thoughts of peace, and not of evil, to give you an expected end." I am honored to be alive to share my experiences with people, and to show mankind that I serve a loving God who is in control of my life and the lives of those who believe in Him.

This God will "show up" with all power in His hands.

This God will fulfill His divine purpose for each of us, as we experience Him in our personal 25th hour situations.

We have plans, but God is the ultimate planner. Give Him a chance to get into your life and plan it. Seek Him first and all other blessings will be added unto you.

God's plan for your life is this:

God's

P urpose

L iving (through you) to

A ffect your

N eighbors. Your life can affect others. **The PLAN** is for you to begin at home then branch out to your neighbors. The life you live should extend into the community, town or borough, affecting the neighbors. It should then extend to your city, state, parish or province, ultimately affecting the nation.

Your life's purpose goes beyond the mundane, routine, nine-to-five job upon which you so faithfully depend. There is much more to your life than the degrees lining the walls of your office or home. Sure, years of diligent studies have paid off, thank God! You have earned the position at the hospital of your choice or the position you so desperately wanted at the Fortune 500 Company. But where is God in all this? How does He factor into your life? Have you forgotten, or maybe you did not know, that it is God who *gives* and it is God who *takes* away (Job 1:21b). God made some investments in you, and He is very interested in reaping the dividends now. Consider what you will do. Continue to live by your plans, which are doomed to fail, or trust **the PLAN** of God that is guaranteed to succeed. I encourage you to seek after the latter.

Hector and Veronica made plans without seeking the counsel of the Lord. However, God supernaturally interrupted their plans to make room for what was to unfold in my life. Satan could not physically remove me, and so he tried to emotionally cripple my young mind. God was watching. He cares and is very much interested in the divine arrangements He strategically placed on this earth, you and me. One arrangement God had for me, was a man by the name of Roderick Richardson Caesar.

Chapter Two

THE FELLOWSHIP OF HIS SUFFERING

Roderick and I sat patiently in the doctor's office waiting for the receptionist to call my name. I was not anxious, but I knew that Doctor Henderson would not be pleased with the results of the test. Although I was composed and had a strong resolve to trust the Lord, I could not help but think of the two previous miscarriages that plagued my mind.

I am married to a man who has no brothers to assist in carrying on the Caesar lineage. His father's brothers and sisters produced no siblings at all, and even his sister, Beverly, had only one child - - a daughter, Rhonda. The son had to come through us. We brought two beautiful girls into the world, Naomi and Lydia, and realized that the Caesar name could be perpetuated through our daughters. After two normal full-term pregnancies, there did not seem to be any cause for concern when I got pregnant for the third time. The only mentionable challenge I recalled was that during my second pregnancy with Lydia, I was hospitalized in the eighth month. After a routine checkup, the doctor realized that my blood sugar level was dangerously high with a reading of over 400. I was immediately hospitalized for a week to control the gestational diabetes through diet. Knowing the importance of obeying the doctor, I stuck to the 1800 calories per day until three weeks later when I delivered by Caesarean section, an active eight pounds four ounces baby girl.

I had a desire, or you may call it a press, to have a male child, so two years after Lydia's birth, I got pregnant again. This third pregnancy began quite normal until I entered the fifth month. I remembered being in Bible Study one night at church and felt queasy in my stomach. I left word for Roderick that I was heading home because I was not feeling well. At home the feeling intensified and I chalked it up to the dinner I had eaten, to be exact, the pickled beets! Regurgitation ensued confirming in my mind that it was what I had eaten. However, I began to feel feverish, but did not in any way feel that the baby was in danger. I had visited the doctor for a check up that very evening, and everything appeared to be fine. The vomiting intensified and I thought to myself, *with such violent pukes, I hope the baby is okay.* When Roderick arrived home, I was still ill and he inquired if he should call the doctor. I advised against it because the check up showed that everything with the baby was all right. Nonetheless, I had a rough night, and by five o'clock the next morning I began experiencing severe abdominal cramps along with bleeding. This time we called the doctor, and within two hours I was delivering a still - born baby girl who had died in my uterus within 14 hours after a routine checkup! This was a painful experience physically and emotionally.

The doctor's conclusion was that fibroids interfered with the baby developing to full term. I delivered the dead child, and watched the doctors, nurses and interns examine the baby to pinpoint the cause for the miscarriage. I overheard them talking about the underdevelopment of the fetus, and remarked that even if the fetus went full term, she would be premature in size. They concluded that the baby's competition with the growing fibroid ended in the loss of her life. I wept before the Lord and asked him to heal my uterus of those nuisance fibroids. Surgery was not offered as an option, because the doctor felt my body needed time to heal before endeavoring to have a myomectomy - - the surgical removal of fibroids from the uterus. Emotionally, I was devastated, but embraced with thanksgiving the two beautiful girls the Lord had already given to me.

Eighteen months later, I conceived again. This time I was immediately placed on bed rest after being scolded by the doctor. He felt I was "a glutton for punishment" coining a Jamaican expression. Doctor Henderson indicated that those bothersome fibroids, although they shrank after the first miscarriage, intensified in growth during pregnancy. They were interfering with the fetus, thus creating the challenge for a full-term pregnancy. With legs elevated and a housekeeper on call, I stayed put! No sonograms, no prenatal examinations, and no stair climbing. The doctor feared that too much exertion would shorten the possibility for a full term delivery. He was waiting for me to get pass what he called "the critical months." Nevertheless, five months into this pregnancy I lost the baby. This time the pain was excruciating and unbearable. It felt as if my insides were being ripped apart piece-by-piece. The bleeding was profuse and superabundant. Rushed to the hospital, I was given immediate attention and this time, with local anesthesia, the fetus was dislodged. Due to the nature of this miscarriage, the sex of the child was not known. Upon inquiring, I was told that the baby was so mangled they were unable to identify the sex. There was speculation that it was a boy, but no one knew for sure.

I questioned the Lord concerning the manner in which this baby was taken from me. After much prayer and deliberation, I concluded that the God of this universe allows circumstances and experiences to come our way to draw us closer to Him; to know "the fellowship of His suffering"(Philippians 3:10).

What a paradox.

A loving God allows us to experience pain because of His love for us.

Imagine this, if you will. Jesus had already borne that pain for me on the cross and even more excruciating pain. He was beaten, scourged, thorns placed on His head, nailed to a cross, and His side pierced with a sword. Pain I will never, ever experience, comprehend or even fathom. But the apostle Paul encourages us to "know" Him in Philippians chapter 3, and in knowing Him, we will encounter pain and suffering.

Pain is an inevitable part of life because of the sin of fallen man. This condition was brought about because of disobedience in the Garden of Eden. When mankind disobeyed God, He threw them out of a "pain-free" garden and placed them in a world full of pain and sorrow. In Genesis 3:16, He told Eve ". . . in sorrow shalt thou bring forth children. . ." hence, the pain I experienced was a result of the sin of my fore parents. However, God had a plan of redemption for mankind before the foundation of the world, which would free us from the bondage of sin and death. Through His only Son, Jesus, my penalty for sin was paid for on the cross of Calvary - - what a blessing! I would still, however, experience the pangs of childbirth as long I am in this flesh.

The physical and emotional pains of miscarriage brought me into a simple understanding and knowledge of the Lord that I did not have before. Live long enough and life will teach you lessons that will reveal who Jehovah really is. His love for me sent Jesus, His only Son, to take my place on the cross. I was guilty of death, because the Bible states that the wages, (penalty, earnings, result) of sin is death, and as a sinner, death was to be my portion.

The scripture continues to state that, the gift of God is eternal (everlasting, unending, timeless, perpetual,) life through Jesus Christ our Lord (Romans. 6:23). Because of Jesus' sacrifice for me on Calvary, I have abundant, everlasting life. Praise the Lord! Therefore, after reading Philippians 3:10, "that I may know Him, and the power of His resurrection, and the fellowship of His suffering. . ." for the first time it dawned on me what that Scripture really meant. I gained a level of appreciation for the Lord that took me to a new height of comprehension. My physical pain could never measure up to one iota of suffering the Lord endured for me on that momentous day when He uttered, "It is finished!"

If you have ever had your heart broken by a spouse, a child, a sibling, a friend or even a leader, Jesus understands - - He was there. If you have grieved over the death of a loved one or had to bury a baby after a stillborn delivery, the Lord felt that! The experience of dejection, rejection and subjection to the unfairness of life are not unknown to the Lord - - He's been there. Your feelings of brokenness, heartache, failure, and or disappointment were all laid on Jesus at Calvary. The prophet Isaiah declared in chapter 61 of his book that the Messiah would come "to preach good tidings unto the meek. . . . to bind up the brokenhearted and to declare liberty to the captives . . . to give unto them beauty for ashes, the oil of joy for mourning and the garment of praise for the spirit of heaviness. . ." and that He did! He felt the needs of the people and was moved with compassion for them.

In the gospels, we find the Lord Jesus fulfilling Isaiah's prophecy as He walked on this earth. He wept over Jerusalem, opened the eyes of the blind, straightened the back of a woman who was crippled for 18 years, freed a woman from the penalty of adultery, cured leprosy, cast out demons and dried up issues of blood. He mingled with the poor, the outcast and the forgotten. He gave them "beauty for ashes, the oil of joy for mourning and the garment of praise for the spirit of heaviness." He demonstrated to the Pharisees what true love was all about. He spoke authoritatively with power and conviction. He pointed people to His Father, Jehovah, by completing the purpose for which He came. He voluntarily took upon Himself the sins of the whole world - - yours and mine. He took it all.

I am part of a group of people, united in relationship with Jesus, sharing in the "fellowship of His suffering." I may not be penning this memoir from behind the bars of a physical prison, but I know how it feels to be in a prison of emotional suffering. I reached out and received my "beauty for ashes" and I purposefully and deliberately put on the *"garment* of praise." He bought those liberties for me, and by His grace I will appropriate all of them.

Also, I am, by faith, sharing in the resurrection experience to come. Not only have I a hope of a future resurrection, but also I have already experienced emotional resurrection. In order for resurrection to take place, something has to die. I had to die to myself - - particularly to my self-pity. God was offering me hope, but I had to reach out and grab it - - and that, I did. It was Jesus who stated to Mary and Martha at Lazarus' grave that He was "the resurrection and the life"(John 11:25). What a powerful connection we have through Christ Jesus. There isn't anything man can offer me in exchange for this everlasting, unending, personal relationship with Jesus Christ. Once I obtained my emotional resurrection, I was able to move on with living. Additionally, I am also certain that my two little ones will one day experience the resurrection unto life, when the Lord returns for His saints (1 Thessalonians. 4:13-17).

Contrary to some medical opinion, I know that life begins at conception. Therefore, I have two babies in glory. Sure the miscarriages were devastating and disheartening, but life was out of my hands and in the hands of the Almighty. Having two children at home helped to ease the emotional pain. However, carrying a child for five months, feeling the movements and the kicking of the fetus, offered some level of hope to our family. Not only was Roderick hopeful for a healthy child, but also Naomi and Lydia often felt the movement of life inside my body and they, too, hoped for a healthy brother or sister. It appeared, though, as if the odds were stacked against me to have a male child. Dr. Henderson urged me never to try again, but to be happy with the two healthy girls I had at home. I realized one thing. I serve a God who is too loving to be unkind and too wise to make mistakes. And so, when I assured the doctor that I would try again, he strongly advised against it, "Oh, no," said Dr. Henderson. "No more children for you. Another pregnancy could lead to more complications and place your life at risk. Would you want that for your wife?" he questioned Roderick. He continued, "Enjoy the two girls and dispel from your heart and mind the desires of having a boy. Your uterus is in such a poor and unhealthy condition, that I suggest you consider a hysterectomy."

Before Roderick and I got married, a gynecologist, who examined me, informed me that there were fibroids on my uterus. "If you have any plans of having children, I highly recommend that you have them removed as soon as possible," he offered. He assured us that removal was the best option, and at my age, time was of the essence. Immediately after our honeymoon, I went into the hospital and had a myomectomy. The doctor indicated that all my children would be born by Caesarean section because of the incision on my uterus, which could potentially rupture during childbirth. I always wanted to have my children naturally, as I watched my older sister, Sandra, so beautifully give birth to her children.

This was a dream I abandoned and just thanked God for the possibility to bring children into the world. Roderick was satisfied with the girls and strongly assured me that he was not "caught up" with having a son. "Sure it would be wonderful to have a son, but not at the risk of losing you," came his honest reply. I could not shake the overwhelming drive to trust God for a miracle and believe that He would bless my womb once again with a son. I asked the Lord to honor my husband by fulfilling my prayer, and also to reward my father-in-law, Bishop Roderick R. Caesar, Sr. by allowing him to hold a grandson before he closed his eyes in death. I was in a hurry, but the Lord certainly was not.

As we waited to be called, my mind again was flooded with questions. *Will I lose this one also? Am I going to be on bed rest for the full term of this pregnancy?* Certainly the Lord healed my womb therefore I had nothing to fear. I was confident that my womb was healed. As immediately as the thoughts inundated my mind, the Lord reminded me of the sure promise He had given to me on Friday, December 7, 1988, at Bethel Gospel Tabernacle.

Chapter Three

BREAKTHROUGH!

After my second miscarriage, I began to spiritually drift from the Lord, and doubt began to set in. I had plenty of time on my hands and as the saying goes, "Idle time is the devil's workshop." I became spiritually complacent and disinterested in the things of the Lord. Reading the Word became laborious, and it appeared as if my prayers did not get beyond the ceiling. I became totally consumed with raising the girls exposing them not only to spiritual things, but cultural and social activities as well. Going once a week to church was plenty; I had an excellent excuse. *Two little ones to raise. I certainly can't spend all my time in church,* I mused.

I was unhappy and felt unfulfilled. Depression crept in and all I wanted to do was stay home. Roderick sensed my "lackluster" deportment, but chalked it up to my needing a vacation. Hence, we took time off and spent a wonderful week at a resort in Florida. The time together was fabulous, but my attitude toward the things of the Lord was the same.

Back at home I engrossed myself with the girls - chauffeuring them back and forth to their extra curricular activities. I kept my hands in their homework, science projects and book reports. I worked from home therefore any interaction with the church office staff was primarily through the telephone and the fax machine. Perfect. No one could read through the facade. That is how I wanted it and that is how it was going to be. I really did not want anyone asking questions and I certainly did not want to give any answers. Complacency set in. I wasn't even sure why I felt so "low." Life was no longer exciting or adventuresome - - I was in a pit of despair. *Was it because of the miscarriage? Was I subconsciously blaming God? Was I blaming Roderick or myself? Was I over-worked?* I could not put my finger on the root of my emotional low.

Communication between Roderick and me was strained. We seemed like two trains heading in opposite directions, full speed ahead. I was not getting the needed attention, nor was I getting the assistance with the children that I required of Roderick. If he opened his eyes and looked around, he could see that I needed help. I pondered to myself - - *I need some help. Can't you see that? Why should I ask you to help - open your eyes, Roderick!* I began finding fault with him and blamed him for my emotional condition. Dislike crept in and soon I began to tolerate him instead of loving him, as I knew he should be loved. I began accepting the compliments of other men and even enjoyed them! *They notice me, how come he doesn't? They compliment me, why doesn't he?*

This really kept me down…

I was in a pit of confusion…

Uncertain about my feelings toward Roderick…

I needed my space…

I needed to be away from everyone and everything.

Yes! A long vacation alone would clear my head. Or better yet, I needed a vacation with someone who would cater to me. Someone to cater to my needs. Someone to cater to my emotions. Someone who understood me. Someone who understood what I was feeling. Someone who could clear up the confusion!

Satan had a stronghold on my mind and I felt like giving up. Spiritual abortion was slowly making its way into my psyche, and I even began to question God's love for me. I questioned and doubted His promises. I was losing control, and it wasn't a great feeling. Satan deceived me into believing that God had forgotten about me and forgotten about my desires to have a son. *"You'll never have a son to carry on the ministry"* came Satan's taunts. *"Look at you. You are five years away from forty, and you know the risks involved with having children when you are over 35. And oh, by the way, you'll definitely miscarry again, so why bother?"* He stayed in my ear gate - - was ever present in my mind - - and I entertained his onslaughts. He even indicated that if God really loved me, He would not "torture" me the way He had been. Torture!

Physical and emotional!

Satan knew that my breakthrough was close, and he wanted to keep me from it, so he turned up the pressure, but...

On Friday, December 7, 1988, Pastor Ernestine Cleveland Reems of Oakland, California, was in the midst of conducting a revival at Bethel. Each night I dutifully attended the services, feeling convicted, but leaving with no change. Her text that memorable Friday night was from Daniel chapter 10: 1-14. She preached about Satan holding up the blessing that God had in store for us.

"I know the Lord heard your prayer when you first prayed, but perhaps Satan sent a demon to intercept the prayer," came her strong and forceful words. She explained to us that sometimes we hold up our own blessing because of fear, unbelief or disobedience.

"Ask God's forgiveness tonight. Release your faith, trust the Lord and watch Him do the rest," continued the resounding instruction through this woman of God.

"Tonight," she declared, "it's time for the old devil to release your blessing, because an angel of the Lord has intercepted the enemy and released the answered prayer into your hands." I knew the Lord was personally dealing with me, because my disobedience had plagued me for months. Even before she concluded her message, with tears in my eyes, I confessed my sins to the Lord, repented and asked to be forgiven. I felt the anointing oil of the Holy Spirit pour over my body. The cleansing process began and I knew God was ridding me of disobedience and rebellion.

Pastor Reems made an appeal for us to come to the altar to be personally prayed for and anointed. People inundated the altar, repenting, weeping, and claiming their blessings. The move of God was powerful in the church that night. She laid hands on everyone and prayed the prayer of faith for their deliverance. Things were happening so quickly, it dawned on me that she had not anointed me or prayed for me. I began to feel discouraged, but the Lord promptly reminded me that He was the one with the anointing, not the woman - - she was simply a chosen vessel yielded to Him. I instantly surrendered my will, my way, my desires, and my emotions to the Lord.

As I wept profusely, I realized that I was in a battle for my life. On the one hand, I could feel the warm embrace of the Lord, and on the other hand, I felt the enemy struggling to keep me in bondage. The striving was great. I ended up on the floor determined to be free from the bondage Satan had over my mind.

I was desperate!

I cried out to the Lord!

He heard me!

My focus was not on those around me, but like Jacob, I was wrestling for my blessing. I dispelled from my thoughts what people might be thinking, wondering or conjuring in their minds - - *look at the pastor's wife on the floor. What's wrong with her? Maybe her marriage is in trouble. It doesn't take all that!* I dismissed every thought and I fought. I had one aim and that was to be free. I was determined, and I desperately wanted to embrace freedom. I completely surrendered to the Holy Spirit's anointing. I felt the burden lift, and a sweet peace swept over me - - the struggle ended.

That night, while I was in communion with the Lord, He made some promises to me that I have held dear to my heart. He anointed me with power. He anointed me with peace. His anointing gave me strength to believe. He softly spoke to my spirit and said, *"I will bless your womb with a male child because I see the sincerity of your heart."* I promised the Lord that when He blessed my womb with a son, I would give him back to the Lord like Hannah did with Samuel. He would grow up to be a man of God. He would walk in the footsteps of his father and grandfather. What a legacy! I meant every word of my prayer. For a moment I felt like Hannah, knowing that God was definitely going to answer my request after all. The tears were unending. I must have stayed at the altar for hours. He continued to bless me with spiritual gifts beyond measure.

The Lord encouraged me to also believe that He had put healing into my hands. Again the tears were continuous. I said a resounding, *Yes,* to my Savior. I was dumbfounded that the Lord looked beyond my faults, saw my need, forgave me and instantaneously began to pour out His grace and favor in my direction. I was speechless. The anointing was powerful!

He also fortified my love for my husband, Roderick, and gave me the assurance that I would, with His help, never again be distracted by the issues and stresses of life that had attempted to sap the genuine love I had for my husband. I began to smile as I thought of the wondrous grace of the Lord to me. I was bursting with excitement as I envisioned sharing with Roderick that what God was doing in my life would have a lasting impact on our personal relationship!

The service had long ended, and I realized that I was left in the sanctuary with about thirty other praying individuals. I noticed a small cluster of people gathered around a woman on the opposite side from where I was sitting - - they were praying for her. I was so engrossed in what God was doing in my life that I paid no attention to the group and their loud appeal to God. A dear sister in the Lord, Maxine Goodrich, approached me and indicated that I should go and pray for the woman - - something about a problem with her leg, and her not being able to walk without a brace. She also stated that she saw the anointing of the Lord upon me, and that I was the one to lay hands on the woman. At first I was reluctant to move, but the Holy Spirit reminded me of the conversation we had just had.

With the power of the Holy Spirit and faith, I crawled over to where this woman was seated. Without looking up at her, I placed my hands on her knees and prayed a simple prayer of faith. She immediately stood up, removed the braces, and started to walk slowly and cautiously, then her pace increased and before our very eyes she began running around the church. It was God through the Name of His Son Jesus, and the anointing of the Holy Spirit, coupled with our faith that did the job. We all began to leap, jump, shout and praise God for the miracle we experienced with our own eyes. By this time it was already about 2:00 a. m. and no one wanted to leave the church. God was working in the lives of His people. I was shedding more tears, amazed at the Lord who honored me that night. He showed me instantaneously that He is in control, and that

His timetable is never too late, but He is always right on time. As in the case of Lazarus, Jesus was four days late, according to man's timetable, but He was on time not only to fulfill a miracle, but also to accomplish His divine assignment.

That night after I arrived home at about three in the morning, tired and still under the anointing of the Lord, He honored my prayer and blessed my womb with His gift of life. I knew right then and there that God's forgiveness is instantaneous, if our motive toward Him is genuine. I lovingly took the time to apologize to my sweetheart for taking him for granted. As I spoke with him, his embrace tightened and he also assured me that God had been dealing with him as well. We recommitted ourselves to each other and vowed to honor the pledges that we made, not only to each other, but also to the Lord.

I was desperate and needed God to perform a miracle in my life. Not only did He cleanse me, forgive me and revitalize my love for Roderick, He also supernaturally healed a woman through my faith to believe with her for the impossible. He continued to extend His grace by blessing my womb that very night with a male child. I knew it, because He promised it to me, but like Mary, I kept those things and pondered them in my heart.

Beverly Morrison Caesar

Chapter Four

FAITH WALK

Before going to Dr. Henderson for his confirmation of my fifth pregnancy, I was approached by my sister, Robyn. Robyn came into my life when she was at the tender age of 13, looking for a big sister. Our kindred spirits linked, and we have been sisters to this day.

Robyn was just beginning to step out into her prophetic gift, and she approached me with a word from the Lord.

"Sissy, you are carrying a male child, and he will come before his due date," came her sure word. "The Lord gave me Isaiah. 66:7 to confirm His word to you; 'before she travailed, she brought forth; before her pain came, she was delivered of a man child.'" She continued, "Sissy, I was talking to the Lord about you in prayer and I felt very strongly that this pregnancy will produce a boy. Before your pain comes and even before your normal time for contractions, your son will be born. The Lord said not to worry, because you and the child will be fine." She spoke with strong conviction and smiled with assurance. I placed no credence in what she stated, because I felt that God had healed my womb, hence, I would take the child full term. It seemed to me that she had only heard "half" of what God was saying. The part about the male child definitely witnessed to my spirit, but the "other" part was not of God. She continued to declare that this would not be the last child either, but more would come from my womb, quoting Isaiah. 66:7-14. *Okay, she certainly went too far this time,* was my thought. Because she was my little sister, I politely listened, but told her that she was wrong about the baby's early arrival, and certainly mistaken about having more children. Her strong resolve was unnerving. I knew that this would be my last pregnancy!

Soon after the examination, Dr. Henderson placed me on immediate bed rest and said with confidence, "I'll just wait for you to miscarry this one as you did the other two." In addition, he suggested a "live-in" housekeeper. It's not that he was cold and insensitive, but as a scientist he was stating the medical facts. With the condition of my uterus and my past experiences, he gave us his medical opinion. But, you see, the God I serve looks beyond facts and declares the truth. In addition, God had made a promise to me concerning having a son. Why then would He perform such a miracle without first healing my womb? This was my personal conviction. Therefore, I rested on truth, not on medical facts! I told Dr. Henderson with godly confidence that I would not lose this baby at all. In my mind, and after the experience I had with the Lord on that Friday night, I believed I would carry this child full term without any complications - - or so I thought.

I was a pro at "bed rest" pregnancies. Feet elevated, bedridden, minimal movement, restricted to the upstairs, no lifting - - simply confined to the bed. For an active person, this was torture. But I had plenty of practice - - two, to be exact - - I was ready! The housekeeper, Ms. Gloria, was summoned to move in and assist. Thank God the bed could adjust for back and leg comforts. The hospital table was brought back to the bedroom, and my computer was set up on the bed for easy access. I still fulfilled my obligations as financial secretary of Bethel, working from the fully equipped room. The doctor waited for another mishap, but I waited for another miracle. Each day my faith waned. Each time I stood up just to walk to the bathroom, I felt the amniotic fluid slowly escape.

I was afraid to go to the bathroom. I began to doubt the promise. The Friday night experience loomed before my mind's eye as a reminder that God was depending on me to trust Him, and not to count on what I saw or felt. This faith walk is one of trust, not one of feelings and emotions. Hebrews 11:1 states, "Now faith is the substance of things hoped for, the evidence of things not seen." If God said it in His Word, then it must be so. But the substance and the evidence appeared to be diminishing, as I believed God for a son. The evidence of what I was hoping for seemed to be disappearing in the bathroom. Sure, I trusted the Lord and sure I believed His word, but sometimes it was difficult to separate reality from trust.

It was through the gospel artist, Carman that I gained the level of trust needed to pass this test. He is one of my favorite lyricists and singers. I played his music in my room on a daily basis because the lyrics of his songs were powerful. One particular song describes faith in this way, "Faith is stepping out on nothing and finding something there." Those words helped to give me the impetus to believe. I had to step out on what I considered nothing - - a child I believed God for, who was waning everyday. I had to know that at the appointed time the child would be **there**, because God was **there**, also!

The Lord also placed a faithful woman in my life to aid in the fulfillment of His promise to me. Our housekeeper, Ms Gloria, was a godsend. Her assistance with the children and her gentle attention to me were paramount. Breakfast and dinner were served meticulously, lunch I skipped, with her insistence that all my vitamins were in fact consumed. At times I felt guilty of the attention I was receiving not only from Ms. Gloria, but also the attention from the children, from my mom, and from Roderick. Here I was, in a condition beyond my control, yet feeling guilty that people had to wait on me hand and foot. I personally had to deal with the guilt - - and quickly! I certainly did not need that unnecessary thought plaguing my mind, causing emotional stress. I began to relax by thanking the Lord for the varied provisions He had given to me. I determined in my heart to praise instead of to complain!

I was humbled by the tremendous outpouring of phone calls, cards, and concern from my church family, neighbors and friends. I was encouraged. "How are you feeling today?" asked the voice on the other end of the phone.

"Not so good," was my immediate response. "I think I'm going to lose the baby. Each time I get up to walk to the bathroom, I lose some fluid. Pray for me." This was the basic conversation that generated on a daily basis. One day, Roderick happened to be in the room when he overheard my lamentations to someone on the phone. He immediately sat me down and shared a life changing thought with me.

"If you continue speaking negatively like that you will definitely lose the baby," was his solemn reprimand.

"Even if you don't feel well, you must speak as if you are well. Death and life are in the power of the tongue" I sat and listened to this wise counsel. He continued, "From now on, when you are asked about your condition, I want you to say, 'All is well.'" Needless to say, I'm a quick learner. But he continued, "Satan cannot read your mind, because he is neither omniscient nor is he omnipotent. Therefore, he acts on what he hears you say. Understand?"

"I most certainly do!" From that moment on, my words were ones of affirmations and positive declarations of "It is well." I took the time to read and study the narrative of the Shunnamite woman who lost her son and was able to state in the light of death, "It is well," (2 Kings 4:26). Her faith to believe God for the hard thing was encouraging. Also, in 1 Samuel 1:10-11, I read about Hannah - - a woman whose womb was closed up by God. She offered a prayer of faith to the Lord; vowed a vow to give her son back to Him. God honored her prayer and blessed her womb with Samuel, who became the first judge in Israel. Hannah and the Shunnamite woman became my spiritual mentors.

Another area in which my faith was challenged was holding on to God's promise to me that I was going to have a son, not just a child, but, specifically, a son. As different people visited me at home, their general words were like this: "Oh, I'm sure this is another girl, you are carrying just like it's a girl." Or I would hear other comments like, "This one is definitely a boy!" An entire family even took the liberty to send a gift to me, and everything in the package was blue. I would be asked on a regular basis what I thought I was having, and I simply responded, "A healthy baby!" My faith wavered from time to time as I was bombarded with the onslaughts of questions, innuendoes, and well -wishers. I trusted the word of the Lord to me, and held on by faith that God would keep His promise and grant unto me . . . a son.

Chapter Five

GOD'S PROMISE FULFILLED

After being confined to bed for five and a half months, approximately 25 weeks, I was scheduled for a doctor's office visit. It was a beautiful, warm and sunny Wednesday afternoon. I was excited about going outside after being in the house for over five months. We ventured downstairs with caution and into the car. Roderick tried to avoid New York's famous potholes, and we arrived at the doctor's office without any major incident. The routine examination seemed okay and I was sent home - - back to bed. Two days later, it seemed as if my water broke, because the flow was so heavy. We called the doctor and he had me rushed to the hospital. After a quick examination, I was hospitalized. Roderick had a conference in Boston and the doctor encouraged him to attend. The doctor assured us that I was going to be all right. My cervix had dilated and the fetus was preparing for delivery, but Dr. Henderson felt he could stabilize the contractions by pumping magnesium sulfate into my system. Word was sent to the church and the Bethel family began praying.

I recalled a nurse's careful attention to my situation, and she observed upon her examinations that I had a urinary tract infection, which could also be the culprit behind the contractions. Dr. Henderson agreed, and immediately they began an IV with antibiotics to ward off the infection. Things subsided for a while, but the baby's heartbeat was cause for concern. On Saturday, things worsened and the contractions were frequent and challenging. The baby's heartbeat was irregular and erratic. Dr. Henderson did all he could to stop the contractions, but to no avail. He feared for my safety and for the welfare of the child. He knew that the baby was too premature to fight through the birth canal, and he knew my uterus was in no condition for the journey. Because this would be my third Caesarean section after two previous miscarriages, he was overly cautious. I told him to contact my father-in-law. He also called the church office and informed them to contact Roderick in Boston and tell him to rush back home. The decision was made to take the baby by Caesarean section. The tears came without invitation, and doubt gripped my stomach. *Oh God, no! Please save this child.*

"Please don't cut me unless Roderick is here," I earnestly pleaded. "I need him here with me. I want him here. He's never missed a delivery, and I don't want him to miss this one." I continued pleading. "We'll wait until he arrives," I concluded. The church office had reached Roderick and they were frantically trying to locate his actual whereabouts as he was taking the Boston shuttle to get home. The doctor was trying to accommodate my wishes by waiting for Roderick. In the meantime he contacted Bishop Caesar, Sr., at home, as he needed someone's consent to perform a hysterectomy. After the Caesarean section, he was certain that a hysterectomy was inevitable. I was prepared for surgery. They wheeled me to the delivery room and passing the nurse's station, Dr. Henderson allowed me to speak to my father-in-law.

"Hello dear," came his soft reassuring voice. "The doctor believes he will have to do a hysterectomy, because he feels this is the wisest thing to do. I told him to do what was best to keep you here. We don't want to lose you." My eyes welled up with tears and my weak response was, "It is well. I am well and the child is well."

I was wheeled into the sterile, cold, brightly lit room, but Roderick was nowhere around. I was positioned for the procedure with tears in my eyes.

"He's coming. Please wait for him," was my insistent plea. "I'm going to be okay. A few more minutes won't hurt." Dr. Henderson loved us. His relationship with Roderick was unparalleled. I remember he even allowed Roderick to take photos of Lydia's complete Caesarean delivery. The photos were so well executed, that Dr. Henderson used them as a teaching tool for his interns at the hospital. I recalled that on several prenatal visits Roderick and the doctor would talk about computers, politics and religion. My husband was adept in his knowledge of computers and Dr. Henderson picked his brain exploring the possibilities for the hospital's technological advancement. He knew I wanted Roderick there with me, but his concern for my well - being and the welfare of the baby overruled his passion. I had a gut feeling that Roderick would show up. I whispered a silent prayer for his safe and speedy arrival. Before I closed my eyes under the influence of the anesthesia, my love walked in. He was scrubbed and dressed for the task. I smiled, held his hands briefly, then drifted off quoting Isaiah 41:10, "Fear thou not; for I am with thee: be not dismayed; for I am thy God: I will strengthen thee; yea, I will help thee: yea, I will uphold thee with the right hand of my righteousness."

I remember, as a single woman, I attended the funeral of a co-worker, Elaine, who died as a result of too much anesthesia being administered during a hysterectomy. It was a sad funeral. Not only did this woman not know the Lord, but her family was also going through a series of lawsuits and litigation. That incident left a lasting and abiding impression on me. As a fairly healthy, single woman, the thought of hospitalization never entered my mind and that incident certainly offered me no absolute assurance that I would escape such a fate if my path encountered surgery requiring anesthesia. Yet it pleased the Lord to allow me to go that route, several times, to remove the fear that had gripped my mind. My initial encounter with general anesthesia was after returning from my honeymoon, I had a myomectomy. It was at that time that the fear of being "put to sleep" besieged my every waking moment. I had the fear of not waking up from the surgery. The funeral of Elaine replayed over and over in my mind. I could not erase seeing her lying in the casket. I needed help. This was getting out-of-hand.

I shared my apprehensions with Roderick and he was able to help me overcome my fears. He pointed out to me that fear was the absence of faith. 2 Timothy 1:7 states, "For God has not given us a spirit of fear; but of power, and of love, and of a sound mind." Since God does not bring fear on us, then the question is, where does it come from? It comes from our minds or from the influence of Satan. Fear paralyzes us and Satan uses that paralysis to keep us inactive and in bondage. This creates tension in our body and stress is magnified, leaving us emotionally drained as well as physically incapable of functioning. Since the scripture states that instead of fear, God empowers us and He keeps our minds sound, I decided to choose empowerment. I chose to function and operate in the soundness of mind. The decision had to be mine. No one else could take those steps for me. I had to confront the fear face-to-face and embrace love, power and soundness of mind. Not only was I now free, but also, the Lord dropped Isaiah. 41:10 into my spirit. This scripture has taken me through every surgery I've ever experienced.

Awakening from the surgery, I opened my sleepy eyes to find Roderick sitting at my bedside. He looked drained and solemn. I fell off to sleep again, feeling the pangs of the incision in my abdomen, realizing that it was indeed over. This went back and forth for about an hour. Roderick waited patiently for me to be fully awake so we could talk. Our conversation went something like this:

"I know you are wondering what you had?"

"Oh no, I know it's a boy, right?" I asked, just above a whisper.

"Yes, but he is quite ill. They had to rush him to Schneider's Children's Hospital to their neonatal unit, since they don't have one here." Schneider's Children's Hospital is a division of the Long Island Jewish Hospital.

"Oh, I thought I could see him." The disappointment welled up in my throat.

"Oh no! He is much, much too small and sick. They had to act quickly," said Roderick with tenderness in his voice I had never heard before.

"Will he survive the transfer? How long is the ride? Is the ambulance equipped to handle such a sick child?" My questions were pouring out like a cascading waterfall.

"The trip should take about 20-30 minutes and absolutely, yes, he will survive the journey. The neonatal medical transport isolette is like a mini - hospital with all the necessary equipment to keep him alive during transit. You should see this 'mini hospital on wheels,' it's incredible!"

"How was he when Dr. Henderson first took him out after the c-section?"

"Well, they thought he would not live because his apgar score was very low - - it was a two!" This score, named after Virginia Apgar, gives a reading of the child's heart rate, respiratory rate, color, tone and reflexes. The range is from 1-10. Under normal circumstances the test is done every five minutes. Roderick continued, "They did not even attempt to resuscitate or intubate him because they deemed the situation hopeless. He was not viable. I began to pray and I asked God to reverse the score. After a few minutes, I asked them to take the test again, and Beverly the score went up to 8!"

"Wow, that must have been great to see." It was becoming difficult to talk, but I needed to know what happened.

"I never saw doctors and nurses move that quickly. They immediately put the wheels in motion. Long Island Jewish Hospital was called. They gave him an incision under his arm and inserted a chest tube in his lungs, and prepared him for the transfer. They were placing tubes and wires everywhere!"

"Oh, my poor baby! How much did you say he weighed?"

"750 grams which is about one pound nine ounces. They say the chance of survival is minimal."

"Boy, he's really small. Not even two pounds? I didn't expect he'd be so small. You mean that even though his apgar score was raised, they still think his chance of survival is slim?"

"Yeah. Dr. Henderson does not give him 24 hours to live, nor does the pediatrician. They both said that the prognosis is grim."

"Well, we know better, don't we?"

"He's completely in the hands of the Lord, and we expect him to come through. But Bev, he is really small. I did not expect him to be so tiny. God has to bring him through this ordeal. No man can. Just by looking at him, I would have to say only a miracle will bring him out."

"Oh, by the way, did I have a hysterectomy?"

"No, Dr. Henderson decided against it. You had lost too much blood. They had to give you a pint, and your body had experienced too much trauma, so he decided against it."

"Wow, I'm glad for that! Not that I plan to have any more kids, but I certainly am glad he used wisdom." Roderick prayed with me, and I drifted off to sleep thanking God for fulfilling His promise. Another attempt of the enemy had failed. Praise the Lord!

Chapter Six

CAN THIS PROMISE LIVE?

The pains in my abdomen were intense as I tried to position my body into a comfortable berth. Early the next morning, after a difficult night, the pediatrician informed me that the baby's prognosis was grim. Being born a 24-weeker came with many challenges. Some of the many concerns were:

Intraventricular hemorrhage - - bleeds on the brain!

Eyes still fused!

Lungs under-developed!

Heart stressed!

And on and on, the list stretched.

He offered no hope, but he stated that the neonatal doctors at Schneider's Children's Hospital were doing their best.

I could not comprehend all the information reeled at me at that time. I could not even fathom what he really looked like. I just could not envision an infant that small. All I wanted to do was to see my child. The tears flowed as I thought of my baby, forced out into this world early and struggling to live. I blamed myself and I blamed Roderick. I thought of all I did to fail God. I thought He was punishing me because of my disobedience. There had to be something in Roderick's past, perhaps, that offended the Lord and this was His way of punishing us.

I questioned the Lord concerning His method. *You promised me a son,* I complained to God. *You did not tell me he would arrive early. You did not tell me he would be sickly and at death's door. This was not in the plan!* These thoughts submerged my mind as I lay in the hospital bed. Because of the urinary tract infection, I was running a fever, and they would not consider discharging me until the fever broke. Also, due to the Caesarean section, the doctor was allowing at least 5 days before I could go home. I wanted to leave the hospital and go to Schneider's hospital to hold my baby!

Roderick was running back and forth between hospitals to check on the baby and to keep up with me. He was worn out. I had time on my hands to talk with the Lord, read His Word and get a focus on what was happening. I needed some answers. I knew what God said to me on that famous Friday night as I repeatedly rehearsed the experience. After much thought and honestly seeking God's face, I realized that in my haste to receive the blessing, I had not tuned in to all the intricate details of what the Lord had said. I had what I call, selective hearing. The Lord did not say He would *heal* my womb, He simply said He would *bless* my womb with a male child. He did not say that the child would be full-term, He simply promised the blessing. That was my interpretation of the promises He whispered in my ear. I wanted so much to experience what I considered a real miracle, God had to show me that His miracles come in all sizes, and through various methods. His miracles come in all shapes, with perfect timing and exact scheduling. "Don't box me in!" says the Lord. But I had done just that. I boxed Him in according to my level of expectation and faith. Once again the tears flooded my pillow as I asked God's forgiveness.

The last thing I wanted to do was to displease the Lord, and I felt that once again I had disappointed Him. My honor and respect for Him were paramount, and I wanted so much to please Him. The Lord forgave me, wrapped His loving arms around me and told me that His love for me went beyond all my faults; "As far as the east is from the west, so far hath He removed our transgressions from us. Like as a father pitieth his children, so the Lord pitieth them that fear Him." Those reassuring words came from Psalm 103:13. God's pity is not one of reproach, but one of grace. His unmerited favor looks beyond our actions and sees the need of mankind. He does not reward evil for evil, but rewards evil with good. What a great God we serve.

After all that time with the Lord, He brought back to my remembrance Robyn's conversation with me. I turned to the Isaiah scripture and read it over and over; *Lord, you were speaking to me through your Word, but I was too blind to see it because it was coming from Robyn.* I wept and I cried. I did not realize that I had that many tear ducts; by now I should have used them all up! After reading the scripture, I recognized that I could have been emotionally and mentally prepared for this journey had I only listened to the words of my little sister. I was too quick to judge the messenger instead of judging the message. I learned two valuable lessons from this experience. Firstly, I should not box God in by my insecurities or by my preconceived prejudices. Secondly, I must stay tuned to the message of God's Word and not become distracted with the individual God uses, but instead hear what He is saying.

In the middle of my meditation, Dr. Henderson walked in to check on me. He examined the incision and asked general questions about my well - being. He spoke about leaving my uterus intact and that if I wanted to, at a later date I could schedule the hysterectomy. Upon concluding his routine examination, our conversation turned to Roderick Richardson Caesar, III. Dr. Henderson held my hands in his, and went right to the point. He was always good for shooting straight from the hip.

"The boy will not live. There are too many complications because he is severely underdeveloped. His development falls between 24 and 26 weeks. What I mean is this - - certain organs are developed at the 24th week marker while others are developed at the 26th week marker. Statistically speaking, boys do not survive when born this prematurely. Girls have a tendency to fare better than boys. I do not want you to hope, because the situation looks hopeless. He is a very, very, sick baby. He is trying to develop outside your uterus in an artificial womb. The doctors at Schneider's can only do their best and then fate takes over, and fate says he won't make it. I know you wanted a boy, but I told you no more pregnancies. I told you to be happy with your daughters, but you had to try for the boy. Well, you got your son, but he won't make it. I'm really sorry." After terminating such a disheartening, honest, medical appraisal, he was about to leave, when I took a step of faith and said, "Dr. Henderson, thanks for your honest assessment of the situation, but I believe with all my heart that *this boy* will live. *This boy* will make it! *This boy* will beat the odds because my trust is in the Lord." Shocked, but not surprised, he smiled and walked away saying, "I hope for your sake you are right, but if I were you, I would not hope, so that I would not be disappointed." And he walked away with confidence.

My body ached after he left. Although I had spoken with boldness, his words rang in my ears as one of authority. I had to hold on to the promise the Lord had given to me. The days seemed longer than normal and time seemed to stand still.

My older sister Sandra, an RN, visited me and as usual checked to be certain that medically I was being treated properly by the nurses on staff. After assessing that all was in order, she began to share with me her prognosis of the infant. Of course she had not gone to see him, but due to her experience in the field, she gave me her medical evaluation.

"Bev, the baby's chances of survival are not good." She stated with confidence.

"You mean to tell me that you believe he will die?" was my outcry.

"All I am saying is that black boys born at 24 weeks do not survive. The chances are not good."

"The doctor said his development was somewhere between 24 and 26 weeks," trying to steer her in a more positive direction. But she stayed the course.

"Just listen to me Bev, please. I see these babies every day. They look like shriveled up little old men. Their skin is prunish-looking and transparent; it's as if you can see all their internal organs. Their vision is impaired and their lungs grossly underdeveloped. I am speaking from experience. They come in and they go right back out - - dead."

"I don't want to hear your experience or your opinion. You of all people should be offering me hope; instead you sound just like the doctor!"

"Bev, I don't want you to hope against hope. Being in the medical field affords us exposure to things like this. I know your faith in God is high, but where do common sense and facts fit into the prognosis?"

"They don't fit! God is bigger than common sense and facts. The baby will live, Sandra. You wait and see." I could not control the tears. She felt badly for upsetting me, but I held my position and did not allow her expert opinion to overrule my conviction. I briefly shared with her my Friday night experience and all the personal confirmation I was given from people and God's Word. She reluctantly conceded and vowed that she would try to believe with me. She also said that she would begin praying that the child would live. We spent some more precious moments together. She made me comfortable, made certain that I ate, as my appetite had decreased. After our little talk, she promised me that she would pray for little Roderick to live. I understood her position, and she began to understand mine. She came with a message of doubt, but she left with a glimmer of hope.

The nurses encouraged me to walk the corridors to alleviate the gastric discomfort and to regain my strength. Roderick and Mommy were on hand to assist, and they took the walks with me on a regular basis. The fever would not break, so I was stuck in the hospital. I longed to see my baby. Naomi and Lydia visited from afar, as they were too young to visit me in the hospital. I would wave to them and throw kisses their way from my hospital room window, and they in turn, returned the gestures from the ground level. I often noticed Lydia's displeasure of not being able to come upstairs and visit one on one. I would watch Naomi, a very effective "mother hen" gingerly coax Lydia into not crying. In addition, the stubborn fever that plagued my body was a deterrent that kept my darlings away from me. The separation from my baby was painful, but even more disappointing was not being able to hug Naomi and Lydia, especially at this time when I needed their hugs. Again the tears came. I could not help it. I missed my family. Sure, Roderick brought me their hugs and kisses, but that just wasn't the same.

On one visit, Roderick brought a photograph of the baby to give me an idea of how small he was. I was excited and could not wait for him to pull the picture out of his wallet.

"He does not look small at all, he looks bigger and even fatter than I imagined. Wow, I thought I'd be disappointed, but his picture has cleared up my concerns!" I said excitedly, studying every detail with amazement.

"The perception is not balanced," came his immediate response. "I don't want you to get too excited, because he is very small. I should have taken the picture against something relative so you could get a better scope of his actual size. I'm sorry, when I took it, I did not realize that you would not have a true perspective."

"Then, he really does not look like this photo? Is that what you are saying?" I asked quizzically.

His expression pained, Roderick replied, "Well, yes and no. In reality he is very small and does not look quite like the photo. You see this photo shows him in the isolette with only the tubes around him. However, if I had placed my hand in the isolette against him you would see how tiny he truly is. Anyway, you'll be out in two more days and you will see him for yourself."

"I know. Dr. Henderson says it looks like I'll be fully free from this fever, so I can leave here by Friday. Roderick, I am so excited, yet nervous about what to expect when I see little Roderick."

"You'll be fine. God has taken him further than what the doctors expected. **They said he would not live 24 hours and he is already working on his fifth day - - that in and of itself is a miracle! He is experiencing the 25th hour! Even if the Lord had taken him *at* the 25th hour - - that one hour would have been a miracle.** Bethel is praying, the radio audience is praying, friends and families everywhere are bombarding heaven on behalf of this boy. It was Pastor Jackson Senyonga, of Uganda, East Africa, who said, 'God does not respond to need, he responds to prayer.' We certainly need a miracle, and it will happen because of the prayers going forth," concluded Roderick with a strong resolve. I rested on that assurance and waited with a praising heart for Friday to arrive. I held on to God's promise to me and rested in confidence that "all is well, and he shall live."

Chapter Seven

OVERCOMING DOUBT

Checkout was a long, drawn-out process. Finally it arrived, and I excitedly prepared to embrace my two darlings with long awaited hugs and kisses. Naomi and Lydia greeted me with the same exuberance as they fought for my attention and threw themselves on my neck. I was enjoying every effort they made to shower me with love. I was starved for their affection, so the dosage was just right. After giving them what I thought to be a justified amount of attention and affection, my shift was aimed towards little Roderick. After securing the girls at home, Roderick and I hopped into the car and headed for Schneider's Children's Hospital - - the neonatal unit. Again, Roderick did his best to brace me for what I was about to face.

"Remember, he is very small and very sick. I know he'll pull through, but right now he looks bad."

"I can deal with that, I'm sure."

"I don't know, Beverly. It has taken its toll on me. I never dreamt we'd have to deal with a child this small."

"And so many other complications. But you know what?"

"What?"

"I believe that this has come into our lives for several reasons."
"You really think so, don't you?" queried Roderick with composure.

"I believe with all my heart that not only was God seeking for my full attention, but He wanted to bring us closer together, and for our family to become a family of faith. And not only that, I also think the Lord wants to show the entire Bethel family that He is still working miracles today."

"You are right. He also wants our church to become a stronger faith believing church. He wants a people who will trust Him for the impossible."

My mind immediately went to his father, Bishop Roderick Caesar Sr., who had to trust God for the current church we now occupy. He often shared his testimony concerning the building of our sanctuary. I learned after many personal conversations with him that he was a man of faith. Even his marriage to Gertrude, Roderick's mom, was a step of faith. Trusting the words of his sister, Bea, he believed that Gertrude would be his wife. You see, he had lost his first wife after a short marriage and was desirous of "finding a wife" after God's own heart. His evangelist sister, Bea, traveled to Akron, Ohio, to speak at a revival and she met Gertrude, whom she thought would be ideal for her brother. The two ladies became friends and eventually, Roderick was told about this lovely single woman who was not only a pastor, but she was a superb teacher of the Word. Roderick needed no other information, but took a step of faith, being led of the Lord, of course, and proposed to this woman whom he had never met! Taken aback at his forthrightness, at first Gertrude hesitated, but not long thereafter, she accepted his proposal!

His faith also extended to church matters as well. When the Lord told him to build our current facility, the church did not have enough money to undertake such a massive blueprint. However, guided by the Lord, he presented the proposal to his trustee board. He was flatly turned down! They thought he was losing reality and one-by-one they left him to his own plans, which they indicated were doomed from the inception. Faith without works is dead, so Roderick Caesar, Sr. put his works in action, and God came through with the financial backing from sources he never knew existed. Donations, gifts and loans came from the north, south, east and west. God orchestrated the course of events that led to the completion of Bethel Gospel Tabernacle upon the faith of a man whose trust was in the Lord and not in man. This warrior of the faith shared other incidents with me that aided in helping to "grow" my faith in the Lord. And so, listening to his son, Roderick, as we drove to the hospital, I realized that our faith for little Roderick's recovery was not only personal, but it was also corporate. Bethel would experience another demonstration of the hand of the Almighty as He orchestrated this event.

Roderick did his best to prepare me for what I was about to encounter. While in the elevator, he repeatedly asked me, "Are you ready?"

"Sure, I m ready," was my impatient respond. *Does he think I can't handle what I am about to see? Can it be that bad? His photo didn't look so bad after all? Well, I'll just brace myself for the worst!* The questions and the thoughts imploded in my mind. Only one way to deal with all of this - - just face it!

I recalled a faithful sister in our church sharing some precious information with me that encouraged my heart. This woman worked at the Long Island Jewish Hospital. Every day for as long as Rod was in the hospital, she went to the neonatal floor and made her way to the double swing doors to quietly pray for my son. This she did, sometimes three times a day. Mrs. Theda Campbell knew the value of prayer. I thought about this woman and her abiding faith. This gave me the courage and confidence to face the situation with assurance.

We arrived on the fourth floor, neonatal unit, signed in with the receptionist, scrubbed and robed. The unit opened through two swinging doors leading straight into another world. A world of sick babies, babies with all kinds of medical challenges. There were babies of all sizes, some too tiny for a world outside the warmth of a mother's uterus. Others appeared normal in size, but had underlying problems not noticeable to a novice. There were babies of all nationalities with tubes everywhere - humming and buzzing machines. The unit had a clean sterile ambiance with nurses tenderly caring for infants totally dependent on them. Babies rushed out into a cold, foreign and callous world - - a world trying to keep them alive. A world still learning and trying to understand what it must do to keep them breathing. Some babies were breathing without assistance; others were intubated and fighting for life. For me, the sight was alarming.

There were three rooms divided by doorways that opened into each other for easy access. The first room we entered was for the critically sick children. The next room housed the babies who had progressed to serious, but hopeful, and the final room was for those recovering and looking to go home. Doctors were probing, reading charts and making entries. Some were answering questions of concerned parents whose eyes were obviously swollen and puffy from crying or from lack of sleep. Doctors were also on call for emergencies, surgeries and prepared to even be the bearers of bad news. Roderick took my hand and led me to "our isolette" which was in the first room. Little Roderick, "my son," was part of "that" world, laying in an isolette dependent on man and machines to keep him alive. He was part of a growing number of preemies who were given every possible chance to survive with the advancement of technology and research.

However, what I encountered will linger in my mind's eye for eternity. He looked absolutely nothing like the photo Roderick had taken! He was presently weighing only one pound - just about 530 grams - and was a sight that would break any heart. He was transparent, very, very, thin and frail. He was lying on a small, rectangular, white and fluffy sheepskin swatch (lamb's wool), just large enough for his size (see photo on page 80). The isolette was lined in foil, to insulate and keep him warm. There was an eye patch over his eyes to keep the light out, because his lids were still fused together. Needles and tubes were everywhere. There were leads to his chest to measure his heart and respiratory rate; a pulse oximeter to measure his oxygen saturation; an IV catheter to feed him fluids and an orogastric tube so that he could be fed through his stomach. He began with 1cc of glucose for a day and because he tolerated the feeding, 1cc of Similac was introduced. The nurses were encouraged by his rapidity in tolerating the Similac.

He was intubated because his lungs were underdeveloped. He could not breathe on his own. This tube was placed up one nostril and taped to his tiny cheeks to keep it stable. He looked absolutely uncomfortable! I looked closely and noted that his heart "was beating" under full control of a monitor that "watched" his heart rate. Any unusual occurrence would cause the machine to beep, immediately arousing the attention of the nurse. It was not unusual for preemies to stop breathing for no apparent reason, and they had to be aroused by tactile stimulation - - a gentle tap, or massaging of the foot bottom. Oh, how I wished I could take his place! I began to hear my sister's words resound in my ears, *"He will not live."* The words were plausible, almost believable! I could now clearly understand why she did not want me to hope! My thoughts came with doubt. *How can someone so small and so sick survive? He looks worse than she described. No, this cannot be. I must be at the wrong isolette.* I read the birth card carefully. I checked the name, date of birth and realized that this was really my son! My faith wavered and doubt set in, all because of what my eyes were seeing. This time the tears were as large as golf balls and they were unending. Roderick did his best to console me, but to no avail. I could not believe what I was seeing. His head was no bigger than a small plum, yet full of hair! His fingers were like straight pins and his limbs the size of my fingers. I recalled taking off my wedding ring and sliding it up his hands and onto his shoulder! *How can this boy make it? God, what have we done to deserve this?* My mind was in a tailspin and I needed some answers - - fast!

God in His infinite wisdom knew at that precise moment I needed some encouragement. What I saw next shifted my posture. This tiny, little boy began to move and stretch. When I saw those skinny legs stretch out and his arms doing the same in a "gymnastic type" move, I was "blown away!" *"Look at him move, Beverly,"* I could hear the Lord whisper in my ear. *"There is lots of life in him, just trust me. Trust not what your eyes see, because they will fail you. Look through the eyes of faith and remember my promises to you."* The Lord was right there with me to bring my focus into perspective. "Yes, Lord, I will trust you," I responded audibly and Roderick concurred. "Do you want to sit down?" the nurse asked, her tone gentle and full of concern. She had obviously noticed my shakiness and a wastebasket filled with my spent tissues. "No, thank you," I replied with confidence. *How could I sit? I have to see this boy closely and clearly.* I stood and observed him for a long time, realizing that a miracle was unfolding before my very eyes; believing God on one hand and fighting off doubt on the other. I was weeping and questioning, believing and doubting. My faith was vacillating back and forth. My emotions were in a dither, and finally I had to sit down. Roderick sat beside me, but it was as if he wasn't even there.

The doctor came in, introduced himself to me, and gave us an update. Through eyes of unceasing tears and ears cluttered with my own thoughts, I heard him say, "His weight loss is normal, as babies lose ten percent of their body weight during the first week of birth." *Ten percent? That's a lot when this baby only began with one pound nine ounces. I never noticed the weight loss with Naomi and Lydia!! But wow! look at this kid. He can't afford to lose not even one ounce, much less ten ounces!*

"But don't be alarmed, this is quite normal and in a few days he'll begin to put the weight back on." I heard the doctor say as my mind refocused. "It is unusual for a black baby boy born this premature to respond so positively as he has. You know, statistics tell us that little black girls fare the best and then white girls. Black boys are next in line with white boys picking up the rear. However, your son's push for life is very encouraging. Babies this premature normally need surgery to clamp their heart valve shut - the patent ductus artenosus, but his valve closed on its own!" My ears perked up and I found the strength to ask my first question.

"So he should be out of the woods soon, right?"

"Oh no, please don't get your hopes up. He is still very much in the woods. In this hospital, we take it one day at a time. It's too early to tell what the outcome will be. Tomorrow we may find that he has intracranial bleeds or some spinal malfunctioning, which could lead to cerebral palsy. Spinal taps are to be done to rule out meningitis. Blood work is constantly done to check for infection. His lungs are very underdeveloped and only time will take care of that. Also, with his vocal chords paralyzed, he may never speak, so please, take this on a day-to-day basis. His chance of survival is still way below the 30 percent mark. Normally boys born at 24 weeks do not live past 24 hours and he is on his seventh day, so that's encouraging." He paused to adjust little Roderick's apnea monitor, which had beeped.

"Additionally, experience has shown us that even if he makes it, there will be many challenges such as, vision and hearing problems, speech impediments, cerebral palsy, which shows up later after he develops. We have to keep a close watch on his lungs, heart, kidneys, liver and the list goes on. Keep in mind that he is developing outside the confines of your uterus, therefore he is depending on our medical assistance to walk him the rest of the way. Mrs. Caesar, I know this is a lot for you to handle in one night, but I am sure your husband has been keeping you informed as I have been answering all his questions. Try not to absorb everything tonight. I know this is too much for you. My suggestion, as I tell all parents, is not to rush the process. Allow time to take its full course to continue the development. He was three months early, therefore, he needs at least that much time to arrive at what we consider normal. And then he will need at least another month to acclimate to his new world." All that information rolled off his tongue with gentle ease as he was accustomed to sharing with families the challenges that were set before them. I am certain that this routine for him was not altogether pleasurable, but he was gracious in his discourse.

Hope began to soar in me, and I felt strength rise up in my spirit. Although I was crying, my tears were now tears of joy. I began to bless the Lord for this precious miracle. I began to thank Him for answering my prayer and granting me a son. I stood at the isolette with my hands through one of the portholes and caressed his tiny arm and committed him to the Lord. *Lord, I will not wait until I get to Bethel to dedicate him back to you, but tonight, Friday, June 10, 1989, I place my son in your hands - - I give him back to you. Satan wanted to abort this plan, but again you intervened. Thank you for stopping the hand of the enemy. This boy shall live as you promised. A boy destined to serve you and to proclaim you for the rest of his life. He shall be like Samuel, a prophet over the house of the Lord and like Daniel a prophet for the end times. Give him a hunger for the things of God and a desire to please you. Give to him the humility of his grandfather and the wisdom of his dad. Lord, thank you for hearing my prayer and for blessing my womb with this precious gift. I give him back to you tonight.* No one heard my prayer, as I had prayed just above a whisper. The Lord and I knew that He was keeping a record of my prayer and would one day bring it to fruition.

Hospital Days

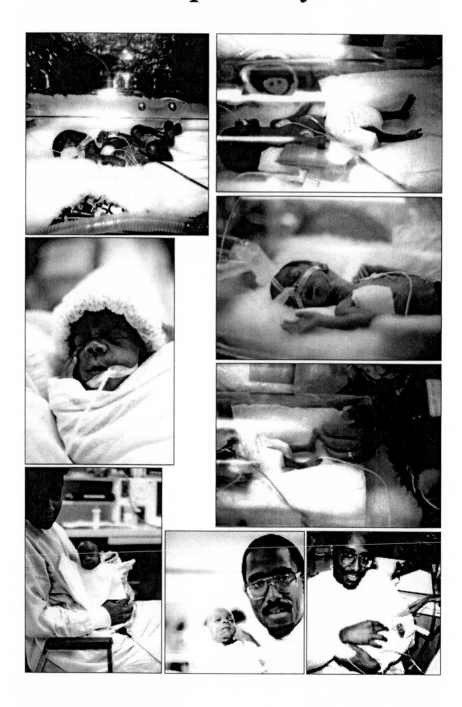

Home At Last

No More Trachea Tube!

Teenage Years

Chapter Eight

THE UPHILL STRUGGLE

We rode home in silence. With the window down, the warm spring air was blowing softly across my face. Roderick sensed my meditative mood and afforded me the solitude. The overwhelming question that harried my mind was simply, what have we done to deserve this? As people, if we are honest with ourselves, at times we question God's doing. It is not a matter of distrust, lack of faith or even disrespect, but simply a flaw in the flesh. This flesh is selfish, self - gratifying and it can be self-destructive. A mental or emotional disturbance may cause insomnia or even paranoia. Trying to cope with the many strains of life can cause stress on our physical bodies, hence we should take heed to the signals.

Because our spiritual walk is a day-by-day experience, it sometimes becomes difficult to look past the challenges in our way and see the victories ahead. To *flesh* out the Word of God is not an easy task to accomplish. The Bible says in Galatians, that Christ should live this life through us in such a way that faith is exemplified; "I am crucified with Christ: nevertheless I live; yet not I, but Christ liveth in me: and the life which I now live in the flesh, I live by the faith of the Son of God, who loved me and gave himself for me." Galatians 2:20. Consequently, as we endeavor to live this life like Christ, the challenge becomes great. Why then the questions? As individuals, we look for some kind of conclusive rationale that offers us answers to the issues of life. When we cannot put our finger on the mark, the questions then become increasingly intense. We expect certain things in life to unfold according to what our minds conceive based on past experiences and even the experiences of others. Yes, we know that God is omnipotent, omniscient, loving and kind.

Yes, we love Him and would not consider leaving the sheepfold. So, why then do we question the unfolding of events we consider unfair or painful, with the, "what have I done to deserve this" question? Each of your answers will be uniquely different, but the essence of the answer is the same. Our finite minds cannot comprehend the infinite God with His plans designed to bring us into a level of obtaining the fullness of *His* divine purpose for *our* lives. We must live this life by faith. His plans for us go beyond our comprehension, and if He would unleash those plans all at one time, we would crumble under the load. "For my thoughts are not your thoughts, neither are your ways my ways saith the Lord. For as the heavens are higher than the earth, so are my ways higher than your ways, and my thoughts than your thoughts." Isaiah 55:8-9. Accordingly, He walks us through His plans one day at a time. As He lives in us and through us, we gain the faith and strength necessary to go to the next level of growth. He also wants to take us from glory to glory. God wants to take us from His glory to His glory. Pastor Jack Hayford in his book, *From Glory to Glory*, writes, "To 'entertain' God's glory is to welcome His workings in our hearts and homes, our churches and congregations, just as we would a beloved guest"(Chosen Book, MI, 1991, p. 24).

When God speaks or whispers a promise to us, His intention is to eventually bring it full circle. The procedure and the process may not be to our liking, but the end result is for His glory. His word is sure, "So shall my word be that goeth forth out of my mouth: It shall not return unto me void, but it shall accomplish that which I please, and it shall prosper in the thing whereunto I sent it." Isaiah 55:11.

Wow!

That's a mouthful!

Straight from His mouth. Who then am I to add or delete one word from His mouth? If God said it, that settles it, whether I believe it or not, and *I choose* to believe. So, the original question at hand was the, *why me?* question but with a *what have I done?* undertone. The answer God gave to me was not so much an answer, but a posture or a position. A posture to stand firm on a position to believe. This is where faith plays a crucial part. God does not reward evil for evil or good for good. He sends the rain on the just and on the unjust. He loves us so much and not only wants to teach us faith experientially, but He wants to take us to a level of hope that will bring glory into our lives, glory into our homes, and glory into our churches. No, He did not bring us to this place because of judgment, but because of love. Certainly we know that we deserve judgment, but His concern for us is to offer us love, a love that we will eventually embrace without question.

I challenge you to position yourself for the journey and learn the lessons well. In this school of life, graduation comes after many examinations and tests. Joseph had to learn his lessons in undesirable classrooms. Do you think he would have registered for those classes? Absolutely not! But God's ways are not our ways, nor are His thoughts our thoughts. God positioned him in those classrooms because He knew what the end would ultimately be. Position in this life does not only speak of professional or material acquisition, but a mindset to handle temptation, deception, and even imprisonment. Joseph was positionally placed in those situations, but his posture was one of integrity and trust. God could trust him not to fail. Can God trust you with the test you are currently facing? Sure He can. There are specific lessons He wants you to learn and your present situation is the path that leads to the conclusion of the test. I am sure you may drop the ball, fall down, or even fail, but God says, "Get up, and try again." Satan is often falsely accused for our failures, but it was Paul, who in Romans 7:19,20 said, "For the good that I would I do not, but the evil which I would not, that I do. Now if I do that which I would not, it is no more I that do it, but sin that dwelleth in me."

Recognizing that sin is a constant with which we struggle, then, the daily crucifixion of the flesh becomes a necessity. (Galatians 2:20)

Failure, whether through our own lusts or through the influence of Satan, can lead to guilt or condemnation. This is the position Satan wants you to hold on to, instead of getting up and trying again. You see, he knows that your graduation or your promotion is imminent; therefore he wants to keep you from accomplishing your dreams. However, you must realize that the classroom experience is a requirement for such accolades. God wanted to get me to the place in Him that would posture me to brace what lay ahead. This classroom experience, and particularly this lesson, led me to recognize a loving Savior who is indeed concerned about me. He is also concerned about His divine plan for my life - - a life that would ultimately affect the lives of others, going from glory to glory.

I was looking forward to the first night at home. To sleep in my own bed and to rest in the comforts of my own room was inviting. The girls were soundly asleep. After looking in on them, praying for them and placing kisses on their tempting cheeks, I decided to retire for the night. Sleep evaded my eyelids, so I paced the floor. Prayer was attempted, but eventually graphic thoughts overpowered the presence of the Lord and I became apprehensive. The sight of Roderick III and the doctor's discourse about his fight for life would not leave my mind. *What if he becomes blind? What if his lungs do not develop and he becomes permanently dependent on the respirator? What if he never speaks? What about his heart? Will he need surgery? Will he be mentally normal?* The questions were unending! I finally decided to pull out Dr. James Dobson's book, **When God Doesn't Make Sense**, (Thomas Nelson, 1982) and I browsed through it. The experiences cited in that book encouraged my despondent, questioning heart. I began to thank God for my personal experience, because it did not come close to some of the experiences that I read about in that book. I just began to praise the Lord for life, for blessings, for miracles and for peace. Eventually, the praise turned to thanksgiving and the thanksgiving turned into worship. The next thing I knew, it was morning and Roderick was awakening me from a deep slumber.

The hospital visits for us were a daily, sometimes twice per day occurrence. They were very strict concerning visitors, and only immediate family members were allowed. Grandparents were the only exceptions. Because Naomi and Lydia were so young, they were restricted for the time being. Also, Naomi had gone away to Bethel's camp - - Camp Joharie, for five weeks. As a "mother hen," she was feeling quite left out, but I assured her that in time she would be able to visit her new baby brother.

It was on June 11, 1989 that my parents, who lived in Maryland, took the three-hour trip to pay a visit to their miracle grandchild. I tried to prepare them as much as I could for what they would see upon their arrival. After the usual signing in, scrubbing and donning the gowns, they entered "the world of the preemies." Daddy, being a newly converted Christian, expressed no hope after laying his eyes on his 11th grandchild and fourth grandson.

"This cannot live?!" He pronounced that benediction with assurance, yet also questioning fate. "How can this 'thing' live?"

came his next question. What his eyes saw indicated to him that life had only paid little Roderick a fleeting visit. He was unsure that what his eyes saw was truly a child or still a fetus. Tears welled up in this man's eyes as he closely watched his grandson squirm in the isolette. What he saw did not add up to what he was accustomed to "seeing." This kind of miracle can only be seen through the eyes of faith, as I had had the distinct pleasure of realizing.

I watched Mommy from my peripheral vision and noticed that her hands were placed together in a prayerful pose right under her chin and resting against her chest. She was silently pacing back and forth. I could not see her eyes because the glasses she wore were tinted. I wondered what was going on in her mind. She walked around all four isolettes in the room, observing, looking and watching.

Finally, she slowly walked back to Rod's unit and then I noticed the tears flowing down her cheeks. She did not wipe them away or try to conceal them. Instead, Mommy began to hum a song. "He's got the whole world, in His hands He's got the whole wide world." She then looked at her tiny grandson and sang aloud, but softly and sweetly, "He's got the little, tiny baby, in His hands, He's got the little tiny baby, in His hands He's got *this* little tiny baby, He's got the whole world in His hands."

She repeated that tune until a sweet peace invaded the entire room and we all sensed at that point that God was speaking through that song. She personalized the song, adding her own lines, "He's got you little, tiny, Roderick, in His hands, He's got my tiny little grandson, in His hands, He's got all these tiny little babies, in His hands, He's got the whole world in His hands."

Well, that's Mommy for you! She always saw the bright side of things, and was always singing or humming. She somehow knew that the right song in the darkest hour could penetrate the obscurity and bring forth light.

"Sure, he's small," came her reassuring words as she finally decided to break the silence by speaking. "What did you expect, Hector? He's three months early. Not fully developed to live outside his mother's warm cocoon. Of course he'll live! This is our miracle! This is Bev's miracle! And this is Bethel's miracle!" *Oh, yes Mommy, keep on talking, lady!* Shouted my innermost thought.

"Hector, look at him move; that should show you he is full of life. He looks really small, but in God's hands he will make it. Just wait and see." She continued, "Bishop Caesar needed a grandson to carry on the heritage through his only son Roderick. If they do not have a boy, who will run Bethel?" Mommy was simply trying to point Daddy away from what his eyes were seeing and to see the bigger picture. Daddy was still shaking his head, as if to say, "I don't know, I really don't know." Of course he did not know, only God knew! We spent the next hour talking, sharing and praying. Mommy wrote down the names of all the babies in that room and made it a matter of business to pray for them daily. Mommy's visits were always encouraging. Eventually, after several months, Daddy accepted Rod's fate, and he, too, joined the family with hope in his spirit.

One day upon arriving at the neonatal unit, we were told that they had done the ultra-sound tests on his brain. The results would show if there was any hydrocephalus. Awaiting the results of that test was stressful. Considering what they could find was cause for concern. The result of the test was negative, and they were quite hopeful that he would not suffer from any brain malfunctioning. That long awaited news was very encouraging.

We had the privilege of caressing him while he was in the isolette, but we waited for the day we could bring him out and hold him. "At two pounds, you'll be able to take him out and hold him," was the response we received. But Rod, on a daily basis, would gain an ounce and then lose two. He would gain three ounces in a week and then lose one the next. It was a roller coaster ride as he tried to gain weight and keep it. This was normal, and there was no cause for worry. The two pounds were playing hide and seek. Then there were the blood transfusions, the blood tests, and episode after episode. He would become apneic; he would stop breathing, sometimes resulting in BradyCardia causing his heart rate to drop - that is an episode in action!

Lydia also wanted to visit. Not only did she miss her big sister, but she also wanted to see this new addition to the family. Her prerequisite for a visit was contingent upon two things: Rod's weight gain and concern for infection.

To Lydia those concerns were not her concerns.

"Did he gain the weight yet?" She asked repeatedly. "I want to see him now! What's taking so long? Can't Jesus just put the weight on him quickly so I can go see him?" This was a slow process for her as well, but we patiently awaited the weight gain. Finally the day came when he reached two pounds!

After stabilizing for two days, we were told we could hold him. We were both excited, and hurried to the hospital for this special moment. Our first time to hold him! I couldn't wait. By this time he was wearing diapers. The diapers were so large that his long skinny legs looked like toothpicks protruding out of a stick doll. We watched as the nurse disconnected some monitors, and prepared him for this venture. The ventilator was kept in place along with the apnea monitor. It was amazing to watch as the nurses, with dexterity and precision, attended to the needs of the small babies. They handled them firmly, assuredly, yet gently and carefully. Hands moved swiftly as tubes, wires, plugs and IV tubing were shifted and rearranged. Some babies needed suctioning, while others needed special attention after their surgery.

My heart broke when I visited and found out that the baby in the isolette to the right of Roderick's isolette had gone through heart surgery. He was so tiny. It was unimaginable to envision doctors opening up a chest so small and being able to repair the heart. I gained an appreciation for nurses and doctors that I never had before. They also became our family and we were treated as such.

"It's time," I heard the nurse say arousing me from my daydreams. Rod was tightly wrapped in a blanket and a wool cap was donning his head. The door to the isolette was opened and he was carefully brought out. All we could see was his tiny face, with the ventilator still in place. I held his small body close to my bosom, and wept. Unfortunately, "Kangaroo Care" was not an option at that time. This special care is when the baby is placed on the mother's bare chest and the infant's temperature becomes regulated by the mom's heat. That privilege I did not have, however, I savored what was afforded me and looked into his peaceful, serene face. His eyes were closed, and occasionally a smile would cross his face, and the dimples would appear. He was beautiful!

Life is precious. The feeling I was experiencing at that precise moment was new to me. Having Naomi and Lydia full term, each weighing over eight pounds, had been taken for granted. Feeling his tiny frame lost in the soft blanket choked me up. I did not want him to go back into that isolette.

Roderick did not fuss, although he knew I was being selfish by holding him for such a long time; he knew what I needed at that time. I eventually gave him his opportunity to hold his only son, and I am certain those short moments were special for him as well (see photo on page 80). The nurse said we could take him out each time we came to visit, but only for a short period of time. That was great news!

The next day when we arrived for our visit, the baby had experienced a setback. They had just completed giving him a blood transfusion. Needless to say, I was alarmed at that news and experienced another emotional reverse. *Was it because we took him out the day before? What if he acquired some germs from us?* Another blood transfusion? Why so many? That bit of information was difficult to fathom. A nurse took the time to explain why he needed so many transfusions and how the process worked.

"Full term babies are able to replenish their own red blood cells, but premature babies cannot "retic" or make reticulocytes, that is, make their own red blood cells." She paused to adjust Rod's apnea monitor as he had tugged it out of position. "Because blood is constantly being drawn from the preemies for lab work, their total blood volume is being depleted, that's why we do so many transfusions - - they need them!" she concluded with persuasion. Although he had had three previous transfusions, somehow this one caused an alarm to sound in my head. She cleared up my ignorance. AIDS was also a subject matter on the lips of everyone at that time. I voiced my concern and the nurse was able to quickly dispel my fears. She told me about a remarkable group of blood donors whose diligence in honoring their commitment as donors enabled the hospital's blood bank to stay in good supply. Additionally, the blood was well tested before it was used. I was sincerely indebted to those donors who took the time to aid in prolonging and even saving the lives of so many babies. During his entire stay in the hospital, he had about eight blood transfusions.

One morning, during one of my visits, the nurse spoke directly to me and politely asked,

"Mrs. Caesar, we will have to shave Rod's head and we want to know what we should do with his hair?" She knew that I was keeping not only a journal, but also any memorabilia that was connected to little Roderick.

"What! Shave his head? What for?"

"We've run out of veins for placement of his IV, and his head has good veins," she said without flinching. However, I was speechless and *I* was flinching.

"Veins no where else, uh?" Came my brilliant response.

"It's not as bad as it sounds. As a mater of fact, the veins in his head are quite good. He has not had any brain operations, therefore those veins would work just fine."

"Will it be painful?" I was already feeling the pain for Rod. "No more than if it was in his hands or feet. All the other veins need a rest and so this is a good option."

"I trust your judgment, so do what you must, and yes I certainly will keep his hair." After shaving his head, he began to look more and more like his grandfather - - Roderick, Sr. , dimples and all.

We brought Naomi home from camp and the day came for the girls to visit. The excitement was contagious. On the way to the hospital they were giggly and full of questions. There was non-stop chatter and questioning which continued when we arrived at the hospital.

"Why do we have to sign in?"

"Oh, we get to use the big sink to wash our hands."

"Aren't these gowns too long?

"Why do we need them?"

The nurses knew ahead of time that we were bringing the girls; therefore they were ready for two excited little girls, Naomi being eight years old and Lydia being five. The nurse disconnected some of the tubes and slowly brought him out of the isolette for the girls to hold. It was a joy to watch their faces light up at this bundle. Lydia was first to hold him. Again the questions were firing from all directions, mostly from Lydia. Naomi, like the "mother hen" understood quite well what was happening to her baby brother. "When can we bring him home?" "Why is that tube in his nose?" "What's that tube in his mouth?" "Can I touch his fingers, please?"

The nurse unwrapped him and brought out one of his tiny hands for the girls to caress. "His hand can fit in mine with lots of room left over," declared Lydia. They sang to him, told him about his room, and Lydia proudly declared that when he came home she would take him to school for "show and tell." Soon it was time to put him back in his isolette with all his accouterments in place. The girls wanted to visit every day. They were able to visit him frequently, feed him from time-to-time, with the nurse's assistance, and even helped out in dressing him. I am certain this experience is indelibly imprinted in their memories.

On a daily basis, during our visits, we would learn that he experienced episodes. Episodes frequently occurred as was previously mentioned, keeping him dependent on the ventilator for breathing. Whenever an episode happened, his dependency on the ventilator increased, and blood tests were done to check for infection. Thank God that each time a blood test was done the results were negative. God was orchestrating this boy's life. Yes, He was using modern medicine and the skill of man to help fulfill His purpose; but He was still Elohim, the Eternal Creator, in full control, even in the 25th hour.

Day-by-day new mercies we saw as God walked this boy through his developmental process. We watched this child experience one episode after another without infection and continued growing in the process. As he showed signs of growth and increased lung capacity, they would take him off the ventilator and put him on the c-pap for trial, as this allowed him to breathe on his own. The c-pap were two prongs, one placed in each nostril with a little pressure applied to keep the lungs opened. Although this was a good thing for him, he began losing weight while on the c-pap, because he had to work harder at breathing. He also suffered too many episodes, therefore he was constantly reintubated. Eventually we began to see strength take hold of his limbs and his weakened muscles developed potency.

We knew his lung capacity was strengthening as we watched him cry with fervor. I recalled during one visit we were able to hear his faint cry which was an indication that life was flowing into his vocal cords - - hallelujah! He finally graduated from the respirator to breathing on his own with the c-pap, without the weight loss and without the episodes.

His progress was steady. There was discussion of him moving into the next room. There was even talk about him feeding from a small bottle. The excitement I felt bolted through my entire body. I could not wait for him to feed on his own. Hope of bringing him home got closer and closer as he began to breathe on his own, and weighing over three pounds. It was the greatest feeling in the world to hold him and feed him at the same time. We even had the opportunity on occasion to bring in clothing to "dress him up."

Unfortunately, this ecstasy was not to last very long. Rod was having difficulty breathing and feeding at the same time. While sucking, his breathing was labored and the sounds he made while straining to breathe were cause for concern. The noise was noticeable to everyone in the room. Because his larynx was paralyzed, the sound we heard was the air struggling to pass through his voice box into his narrow trachea. It sounded like a clogged wind instrument failing to produce the desired note. The doctors hoped his airway would eventually widen as he developed to avoid surgery.

They kept a close watch on him. The episodes increased and he had to be placed back on the ventilator to save his life. When this occurred, he would go back into the "first" room. Oh, how my heart broke whenever that happened. Thank God for a strong husband, whose faith and encouragement kept me afloat.

I also thank God for a praying church. Each Sunday we updated our church family with the progress Rod was making. We shared with them the challenges and called on them to pray. We even informed our radio audience with particularized details of what was unfolding in our lives, and they also began to pray. I know that the prayers of the saints reached into heaven, touched the heart of God and kept the promise alive.

One evening, Roderick and I were called into a conference with Doctor Weeks and two other doctors and a nurse who informed us of our options concerning Rod's breathing.

"We had hoped his airway would open up so that surgery would not be necessary; however, we must do a bronchoscopy. This is an exploratory procedure where we use laser to look into his airway. This will let us know if the problem is the trachea or the vocal cords. Depending on what we find we may have to do a tracheotomy," said Dr. Weeks.

"There are no other options?" Asked Roderick. I was too numb to speak.

"Yes. We can have him struggle while feeding and hope that his airway widens as he grows. He needs his energy to grow, not to fight while eating. The widening is dependent on how narrow his airway was at birth, and his was very narrow. Keep in mind that he was a 24-weeker and this comes with problems. We will do our best to minimize the challenges. We believe that the problem may also be the paralysis of his vocal cords, which is not allowing air to flow into his trachea. If this is the case, a tracheotomy is still inevitable. Also, during this struggle to breathe, while sucking he may aspirate on the formula, causing more difficulties. We could place a feeding tube, a *g-tube*, it's called, directly into his stomach through an incision in his belly. His sucking reflex would not be strengthened through this method, and depending on how long it takes for his airway to develop, this feeding process could become messy," answered Dr. Tinsdale.

"A pacifier could do the job?" came my suggestion. "Just like he did when he first began to nipple. Although he was not actually sucking the formula through the pacifier, the sucking sensation was there because of the pacifier, and the feeding tube down his throat offered the correlation for him." Doctor Weeks replied, "Yes, that is so, but now the challenge is two-fold. Firstly, he is gaining weight nicely and he needs more nutrients, so the recommendation is to feed him by mouth. Secondly, the airway is of great concern. This development usually increases with time and growth. We feel that if his airway is narrow, only time can rectify the widening. If the problem is the vocal cords, the time factor may be lessened depending on when they 'kick in." We want to eliminate all the risks involved in his speech development, so a tracheotomy appears to be the best option. As he grows with the trachea tube, the airway will widen. Surely, we can feed him directly into the stomach, but we feel this option will not be the best for him in the long run. With the tracheotomy he'll be able to suck, eat, and breathe with no problem."

The doctors seemed to be leaning toward a tracheotomy, but our questions continued.

"Wouldn't the procedure be too traumatic for a preemie this size?" Came my doubtful inquiry.

"Not at all. This, as a matter of fact, would help lengthen his life. You see, this would take the stress off his eating, and that is an important factor. He could use that energy instead to grow. The incision or cut would be placed at the point where the air entering through this tube would go directly into the lungs without interference and without struggle. The struggle for breathing would be over. He could live a full life in this condition."

"What? His whole life with a tracheotomy?" I proclaimed with awe.

"No, not at all," interjected Dr. Tinsdale, "Dr. Weeks is simply trying to make a point. The point is that this option offers the best hope. Do you want to see your son continue to struggle to breathe? I shook my head to say "no." "I didn't think so. We recommend that you take this route, but the decision is yours. You cannot delay, because the situation is critical and your son's future rests on the decision you make." Dr. Weeks and the other doctor concluded the verbalization and graciously dismissed themselves.

Roderick appeared to be comfortable with the decision and was certainly more relaxed than I. I marveled at his composure. His faith walk was certainly more consistent than mine was. In my mind, I was already envisioning a catastrophe. However, I really did not think that God would allow this to happen to our son. I was confident of that fact.

A few minutes later a tracheotomy specialist walked in to offer counsel. "I have to prepare you for what I believe is inevitable. This surgery is not the worse thing for your son, actually it is the best thing for him," said Doctor Neomie.

As she spoke, all I could envision was an uncle of mine who had had a tracheotomy. At that time, I was living in Jamaica with my grandmother. This uncle, an elderly man, had a trachea tube because of cancer in his throat due to years of smoking. Recalling the image of the uncovered hole in his neck made me shiver. It was through this hole that my uncle breathed and spoke. I disliked it when he visited us. He was unpleasant not only to look at, but he was difficult to hear and difficult to understand. His speech was guttural and almost inaudible. I was frightened by his appearance. That was the extent of my exposure to tracheotomy. I knew that over the years improvements have been made, and of course, being in America, the great land of research and opportunity, this would not be the case for my son. However, Uncle Winston's face lingered in my mind.

"How long would he have this tube, if we decide on this option?"

"Anywhere from five to seven years." Came the sure response.

"What? Seven years?" Was my uncontrolled outburst.

"Why so long?"

"Well, based on statistics and past experiences, babies in your son's case usually need that much time for the airway to mature or for the vocal cords to develop beyond the paralysis and just kick in." My next response came without much thought or contemplation. All along while the doctors spoke, I concluded that God was not going to take us this route. No surgery and no stomach feeding either. "I don't believe he'll be having the procedure done. He will come out of this state before you know it and the trachea tube won't be necessary." *Beverly* spoke with confidence.

"All we want is the best for your son, and we certainly don't want to go this way. But, if there is no improvement within the next two days, this may be our only option," Dr. Neomie concluded and wished us a good night.

The next day, he seemed to be doing fine on the c-pap. His breathing, was labored while sucking, but I rested on receiving another miracle. Roderick and I prayed for him, and left the hospital.

The following afternoon at approximately 1:00 p.m. the telephone rang, and Dr. Weeks was on the phone. It was not unusual for the doctor to call, because he had done so numerous times before. This time, I hoped his call would be declaring that Rod had indeed come out of the woods and his airway had opened up tremendously. Not so. "We had to do an emergency tracheotomy this morning because he had a serious episode while feeding. Mrs. Caesar, I know you had hoped things would be different, but I'm sorry. This is for your son's best. When you and your husband arrive to see him this evening, he'll be back in the original room in his "old" spot. At this point he is considered critical, so we are watching him closely."

Needless to say, my heart was broken. I politely thanked the doctor, hung up the phone and bawled. *I thought you would heal him,* was my cry unto the Lord. *You promised that he would not have the surgery!* came my desperate plea unto the Lord. *Why, why, why?* I had no other question, but, "Why?" I really thought that the Lord would heal him and I would bring home a healthy five-pound child. I called Roderick, and through my tears and sobbing I related to him the new development.

"Well, the Lord knows best. This is not what I expected, but God is in control."

"Well, I'm disappointed. I'm hurt and I feel as if God let me down!" I replied with honesty. "I knew He was going to heal him and give us a miracle."

"A miracle! We have a miracle. He is a miracle. What do you think this is?"

"I...I know he's a miracle," the words stammered out, "but I was expecting another miracle."

"Well, you prayed amiss," was Roderick's sound reply.

"I prayed amiss? What do you mean?" I felt he was being insensitive to my disappointment.

"You prayed without conferring with God. All you wanted was one thing and one thing only."

"That's not true. You misunderstand what I mean."

"No, I understand you quite well. You hoped for one and only one outcome. You did not consider the possibility that this is what God wanted to do. You did not respect His Sovereignty. You did not open your heart to receive any other way but your way, and that way being - - no tracheotomy. Did you ever consider that perhaps God wants to teach us something from this experience? I am not relishing this trial, but if this is what the Lord wants, I am open o His will."

"Roderick, I am open to the Lord's will, but this? Can this really be His will? Haven't we suffered enough?" That last question did not need answering, because the Lord chastised me right then and there, and I felt the Holy Spirit's tug at my heart.

"You don't have to answer me at all," I confessed to Roderick through tears. "I now know what you mean about praying amiss. I missed God by leaving out a key ingredient, 'Thy will be done.'" We immediately prepared to go and see Rod. We traveled in silence to the hospital as I tried to control the tears. Although I had accepted what was happening, I could not imagine having a child with a trachea tube for a year much less seven years.

Seeing Rod asleep with a tube in his neck was not comforting. His head, face and neck areas were swollen because of the surgery. We were assured that the swelling would decrease by the next day. He did not look comfortable to me at all, but the doctors were quite certain that he was. To think that he was not breathing through his nostrils, but instead through a plastic tube in his neck was mind - boggling. I could not fully comprehend what had taken place, but I had to trust the divine Lord, who in His wisdom orchestrated this course of events. My heart ached and I felt like giving up. Not knowing what lay ahead was disheartening. Unsure if I could cope with this overwhelming task disturbed me - - a child with a breathing tube in his neck? Could I handle such a task?

Chapter Nine

HOME AT LAST

During the consultation with the doctors, we were informed that the episode Rod had was life threatening, therefore their immediate decision was to do a tracheotomy. I finally concluded that they acted in his best interest.

Where do we go from here?

Can his life be normal?

Would the tube interfere with his eating?

What about his vocal cords?

Would this impede the development of his larynx?

Would his voice- box remain paralyzed?

The doctors were patient with our questions. His life would be normal with a few minor adjustments. Nurses at home twelve hours per day. A nebulizer machine humming away connected to six feet of tubing. Suction catheters with saline droplets on hand. The tracheotomy would not interfere with his eating and only time would heal his paralyzed vocal chords. "If everything progresses normally, he could eventually make sounds around his trachea," said Doctor Weeks with hope. "But right now, let's concentrate on getting him up to five pounds and teaching you how to work with this tube in your son's neck."

I was beginning to mentally adjust my psyche to this massive change. Rod began feeding and breathing without any difficulty after the tracheotomy. His development improved rapidly and his progress was impressive. I was certainly glad that this procedure proved to be for his betterment. God knows best and sometimes our faith wavers because we tread on unknown territory. If we depended on our five senses to lead and guide us, we would fail. Proverbs 3:24 tells us that we should not lean unto our own understanding. Sometimes we believe that our understanding of a situation is in total correlation with the Lord's. I was convinced that my understanding of Rod's situation was in agreement with what the Lord was saying - - that he would not have the tracheotomy. But the second half of that scripture is where I failed the test, "In all your ways acknowledge Him and He will direct your path." The only thing I acknowledged was that God was God and therefore His promise was a child without a trachea tube. I did not acknowledge that God was Sovereign and that whatever He chose was best for me and for my son. My reasoning of God's promise, which I thought was faith, led me to hope without true conviction. I was leaning on my sense of "feeling" instead of trusting Him to direct my path.

Feelings can lead to disappointment:
    disappointment in relationships
    disappointment in financial choices.

Feelings can lead to failure:
    failure in our marriages
    failure in our careers

So, beware, you can be fooled by your feelings!

Our judgment becomes smeared and our decision making process becomes flawed. Trust God and not your feelings. This Christian walk is a walk of trust and not a "feeling walk." I am sure many people would agree with me, that if it were left up to our feelings, on a cold winter's Sunday morning, with a warm blanket wrapped around our tired body, we would not venture out from that place of comfort to attempt going to church. The struggle is tremendous! Our minds say *get up* but our bodies feel like staying put! We know our commitment to the Lord is sure-footed, but this morning we are feeling cold footed. Somehow our obedience overpowers our feelings and with a "holy" push we find ourselves showered, singing and ready for church. It does not end there, because the very answer we needed from the Lord concerning a specific situation was given to us during the preached word! Thank God that "feelings" *did* not win... *this* time.

Our concentration shifted as we now had to learn how to take care of a baby with a trachea. We had to learn how to suction him, how to change the tube and how to resuscitate him if it became necessary.

"Resuscitate him? I hope that will never happen."

"You can never be too sure. It is highly probable that during these early months you may have to resuscitate him, so you must learn the procedure well," said the nurse on hand.

"This is more than I can manage, more than what I bargained for. I know this is easy for you because you have done this before, but I don't know if I..." My words faded as the nurse interrupted with a, "Sure you can!"

The nurses were patient with two novices - - one of them, a squeamish mother who never wanted to have anything to do with nursing. (That I left up to Mommy, and my sister, Sandra). The technique of preparing the trachea tube with the string that tied around his neck was quite simple. However, removing the tube and replacing a fresh one in his neck required a certain level of boldness, which I did not possess. The nurses encouraged us to learn the process quickly because Rod would not be released until we fully exhibited all that was required for taking care of him at home.

Immediately, I was determined to master the challenge. I mustered up the boldness I needed to accomplish the task and amazed myself at how "easy" it all turned out to be. The major difference between resuscitating a preemie without a breathing tube in the neck and a preemie with a tracheotomy, was remembering to administer small puffs *into the tube instead of into the nostrils,* and also, using two fingers to apply compressions to the chest area to stimulate the heart was simple to administer. We demonstrated to the doctors, nurses and staff that we could handle the situation. Anything that was needed to make the progress at home successful was closely adhered to, learned and applied. We became pros at handling Rod. The hospital videotaped and photographed us tending Roderick and those photos were used for training in the nurses' program at the hospital.

In the meantime, the buzz phrase at home and at church was, "Little Roderick is coming home!" The prayers of everyone were finally being answered, "The effectual fervent prayer of a righteous man availeth much." James 5:16b. This scripture strengthened my conviction that prayer absolutely changes things. We even re-carpeted the entire house upon the suggestion of the doctors. Carpets in an edifice for over 20 years carried germs and fungi. His room was prepared. All the necessary furniture was in place. A framed embroidered motif, executed by my mom, drafting his name and birth statistics, graced one freshly painted wall. A red, black and white wooden clock announcing his name amidst a baseball, football and sneaker, offered a bright look into the future. A Norman

Rockwell painting of a gentleman reading to children invited you to take a closer look. His room was pleasant, cozy and inviting.

The hospital instructed us to notify our electric company that we were bringing home an infant on life - support, so that in the event of an electrical problem, our home would be on "red alert." Our local police precinct was also notified of this priority case, so they in turn would be on hand immediately if an emergency arose. A nursing agency was contacted to provide care for our son, twelve flexible hours per day. They also kept a close eye on the supplies. I believe that the best nurses in the entire state of New York graced our home as they came and administered professional care for our son.

At last, the day we were all anticipating arrived. We had proven to the entire medical staff that we were capable of rendering excellent care to our son. Last minute instructions were given by the doctors and reminders reinforced by the nurses. After the goodbyes, well wishing and pleasantries, we loaded the car and headed home.

Due to the nature of his condition, we opted that only the family would be there to greet him. Oh what a delight it was to watch Naomi and Lydia fuss over their baby brother. That afternoon Aunt Bev visited. She also expressed joy in seeing and holding her first and only nephew. She remarked at how tiny he was and she was amazed that he was really breathing through the tube in his neck.

"The doctors are amazing," I heard her say softly.

"Why do you say that?"

"To be able to operate on a child this small placing a tube in his neck, one perfect for his size, just amazes me. Also knowing that he is not breathing from his nose, but from the tube further astounds me."

"Yeah, I know," was my response. My mind wandered while she was speaking as my memory took me back to watching the nurses place an IV into Rod's head. *Yes, it was amazing.*

"I'm just glad the Lord brought him through to this point. I'm sure He'll be with you the rest of the way as you face this new challenge," she said, offering hope.

"With the Lord and all the help I have, I know we'll not just survive, but we will do well."

"You know you can count on me in the future. Right now he is too small for me to handle; but when he gets more sizable, count on me. I'm not too keen on being alone with him while this tube is in his neck, but after that, Aunt Bev will be right here." One thing was always certain about Bevy - - her honesty and candor. She concluded, "I finally have a nephew, my only nephew and, I am the proudest aunt in America!"

His room, next to the girls and across from the master bedroom, was fully equipped with all his life-saving apparatus in place. The large 25-pound nebulizer machine with the saline bottle, pumped out moist air through the long corrugated tubing. It hummed with a low, haunting droll. The long 4-foot tubing was attached to a cover that allowed the air to flow directly into his breathing tube. Three times per day, a treatment of proventil had to be administered to Rod to keep his airway loose from congestion and wheezing. The apnea monitor, that kept an accurate account of his heartbeat, was attached around his big toe or thumb and would beep if his heartbeat reached a critical point. An emergency trachea tube was assembled and kept handy just in case we needed to make a crisis switch. Ambu bag was kept near by. This was to be used after suctioning or for resuscitation. The oxygen tank was kept full and ready if needed.

The resuscitate instructions were taped over his crib for accessibility.

Although we had nurses on hand for twelve hour per day shifts, we were left responsible to provide the additional twelve - hour care for Rod. I thank the Lord for providing family and friends who helped us in carrying this staggering load. **Grandma Myrtle,** was a dear woman who assisted in raising, from birth, my husband and his sister, Beverly. She was instrumental during their developmental years and remained close to the family even after their mom's death, and after my marriage to Roderick. When I was pregnant with Rod, she prayed for my welfare and visited regularly, so when the addition to the family came, **Grandma Myrtle** rose to the occasion. She gave her time, attention and care in helping us with Rod and this required great sacrifice on her part. Not only did she become one of the nurses, but she also assisted around the house, and was the official house and family photographer. Her memory lives on in our hearts - - she is really missed.

Another priceless person is Thelma Harty, Rod's godmother. When God made Thelma, He threw away the mold. This loving, caring, compassionate and sacrificial woman is a RN who devoted all her available time to our son. Her ministry to Rod during his critical years has left a permanent imprint on our lives. Roderick and I will never forget the unselfish attention she rendered to Rod.

There are others who gave medical attention to him while he was home and trached. Their sacrifice of love and attention to our son will remain in our hearts forever; my mom, my sister Sandra, my adopted sister, Robyn, and several ladies from Bethel: Virginia Robinson, Kathy Harrison, Coreen Phelts, Shirley Witherspoon, and Rosie Parris. These loving, caring, Registered Nurses helped to ease the stress associated with the responsibility of caring for our son, Roderick III. What a blessing to have a supportive church family!

Thanks Bethel!

Even with everything in place and everyone at their posts, there was one thing missing - - his monitor - - one for his room, and the other to keep with us in the house so that we could listen for any unusual sounds coming from his room. On the day of his arrival home we decided that we would purchase a unit that evening. That was the plan! We had him conformably settled in his room and we gave the girls solemn instructions not to enter his room without permission. Lydia was precocious, strong willed and mischievous. Although Naomi was mature for her age, and reliable, we just wanted to be cautious. But I thank God for her juvenile maturity because it saved her brother's life, his very first day at home!

Chapter Ten

A SISTER'S ALERT

I was just happy to be home and glad to be with the girls. It was late afternoon and the girls were in their room doing their homework. I had put Rod in his small carry seat in a slight upright position and placed the seat in his crib. He looked comfortable and peaceful as he slept. I was downstairs in the kitchen, happily talking and laughing with Roderick and Rhonda, our niece, while sterilizing the bottles. Suddenly, Naomi yelled out, "Mommy, Mommy, something is beeping in the baby's room, and he looks blue!" I quickly dropped everything and scaled the steps with Roderick on my heels. What I saw when I reached his room sent my nervous system into an alarm mode. He was slumped in his chair, his chin completely covering the tube and his complexion was cyanotic - - bluish grayish hue that looked like death.

"Roderick you call 911, and I'll begin to resuscitate him," I amazed myself at my composure. I immediately picked him up, stretched him out on the changing table and with dexterity began the process that I had demonstrated that very morning. I quickly suctioned him and began bagging breaths, using the ambu bag, into his trachea tube and applied two fingers to his chest area.

"EMS is on the way. How's he doing?" came his father's languishing question.

"His heart rate is picking up, but his color is still grayish." I continued the procedure.

"Do you want me to help?" I made room for Roderick but he said, "You're doing a good job, so keep going." I continued the process:

(Remember - - one breath to every 5 compressions).

Small breath!

Two fingers!

Small breath!

Two fingers!

He began to look better as color returned to his cheeks. In about three minutes the doorbell rang and Roderick let the police into the house with walkie-talkies blaring. They entered his room and assessed the situation.

"Your husband told us what happened. So how is he now?" inquired one officer.

"He's doing fine now," I told them.

Good. "When EMS comes, they'll determine if he needs to go back to the hospital," came the reply.

"I don't think that will be necessary. He looks fine, just like normal." My answer was genuinely honest. I certainly did not want him back in the hospital - - not today. He just came home! The tears came and my knees became weak. I had to sit down. I was about to faint - - or so I felt. But I could not sit. EMS arrived several minutes after the call. They evaluated the situation.

"How long was he unconscious?" Asked the technician.

"We don't know. We were downstairs for about fifteen minutes before our daughter called out."

"That's a long time. Let's ask your daughter if she knows." Naomi responded that the beeping was going on for about five minutes - - she wasn't really sure. She thought it came from outside; perhaps a garbage truck reversing. But when the beeping continued, she realized it was coming from Rod's room. She thought we heard it, but when no one came up, she called for us.

"I know he wasn't out for the whole time you were downstairs, but he could have lost a lot of oxygen to the brain. We have to take him to the hospital. Although he is breathing normally and his pressure is okay, we have to do this to be on the safe side. Preemies are known to stop breathing, but they must be aroused immediately. He wasn't, therefore we have to take him."

With police escort, Roderick drove his car while I sat in the EMS vehicle with Rod as he was rushed back to the hospital. Rhonda recalled the look on my face as I entered the vehicle. She describes it as one of dread. A look of, *"Oh God, I hope he is okay. Not the hospital again, please Lord! I just brought him home."*

The emergency room was ready for him. They knew his case well. They drew blood to be tested for arterial blood gas levels, which primarily indicate the oxygen and carbon dioxide levels. Thank God the levels were no cause for concern, nevertheless, I had to leave my child in the hospital and go home to an empty room.

"We have to purchase a monitor tonight," voiced Roderick. We scouted the drug stores and finally bought a unit that was appropriate for our need. *If only we had gotten it earlier, this would not have happened,* I scolded myself. Tears flowed down my cheeks as we walked to the checkout counter. I dismissed myself and pretended that I was interested in an item I had seen. I wept as I walked down the aisle, scolding myself for not securing the monitor as the doctor had recommended. After several minutes, I composed myself, found Roderick and rode home quietly. He seemed contemplative as well. Roderick broke the silence with, "That was some scare we just had."

"I know. I did not feel it until EMS came. Somehow I was not nervous. But after they came in, I felt the weight well-up in my belly. I couldn't stop the tears."

"You were amazing! I'm glad you did the resuscitating, because I might have been too hard on him with my puffs and finger pressure. You were amazing."

"I could not believe it myself. I have to give all the credit to the Lord who kept my hand steady and my focus intact. I did not do it by myself. Thank God for Naomi who was alert enough to call us. She saved his life."

"I'm very proud of her," Roderick replied. I was also proud of our first-born.

Upon arriving home, we assured the girls that Rod was fine and that all he needed was some extra care. He spent two nights in the hospital and came home with no complications. No brain damage and a good strong heart. We positioned the monitor and kept him out of the carry seat, for a while. Satan tried to abort God's miracle, but God had a sister who was attentive enough to keep the plan alive. Naomi was instrumental in God's 25th hour miracle.

A sister who comes to mind is Miriam. She watched over her baby brother, Moses, who was hiding in an ark of bulrushes by the reeds on the bank of the river Nile. (Exodus 3:3-10). As Pharaoh's daughter came to the river to bathe, she noticed the small ark. What if Miriam's response to the princess was different? She was placed in a trustworthy position and passed the test with flying colors. She was not afraid of Pharaoh's daughter. She spoke with boldness as she offered an excellent suggestion.

Although Naomi was instructed not to go into her brother's room, she was sensitive and alert. She recognized that something was wrong and she acted quickly. Miriam also responded in a timely manner. Her suggestion was heeded, and his own biological mother not only physically nurtured Moses, but she also taught him to trust in Jehovah God! God's plan for the future of Israel began to unfold in the life of Moses, although Satan meant to destroy him at birth. Not only was Naomi dependable, she was also trustworthy. Because of her alertness, Rod's life was saved and the plans of Satan defeated.

It is the aim, the desire of the devil to abort the miracles God has for our lives. Developing sensitivity to the voice of the Lord is critical in seeing the plan to completion. Young Samuel had to learn the voice of God, because it was unfamiliar to his tender ear. He also had to learn to know God for himself. Eli, the priest, recognized that Samuel was lacking these skills, so he taught him how to listen and how to respond to God's voice (1 Samuel 3). Unfortunately, as we read in scripture, Eli did not apply these principles to his personal life. Because of Eli's disobedience, God told young Samuel that He was going to destroy Eli's house forever. One thing we must realize is that most of God's promises are conditional - - conditional upon our obedience to Him. We cannot live our lives the way we feel, not comply to the leading of the Holy Spirit and expect the blessings to come rolling in. We should not look for God to bless us if we have not obeyed the requirements. Eli had been warned of God concerning the ungodly actions of his sons, and he, Eli, did not "restrain them," but tolerated their desecration of the house of God. Yes, God is just and full of mercy, but He gives us enough warnings to do what is correct before He allows judgment to fall - - and what a fall that was (1 Samuel 4).

Trying to please the crowd, or trying to please family and friends in order to gain acceptance, confidence, or simply to be appreciated can lead to compromises that will be disappointing. Don't abort your divine blessing for a quick fleeting pleasure that you will perhaps regret the next day. I challenge you not to buckle under the pressure of family to go against God's sovereign will. The influence of people can be very strong, especially if they have played a major role in your nurturing. As you mature in the Lord and become rooted in His Word, you will become sensitive to the voice of God in such a way that the distinction will be clear!

As Samuel matured in his prophetic gift and developed an acute awareness of the voice of God, he was able to lead the children of Israel with clarity. He learned well, therefore God could trust him with a major assignment. I hope that you will develop a sharp awareness of God's voice in your life. I pray that He will instill in you the desire to obey His voice at any cost. I am certain that God's future for you is bright and secure. By God's grace, see His plans lead to completion in your life. After Samuel acquired the skill of hearing from God, he moved forward. Naomi, at the tender age of 8, stepped out into a position of authority to assist in the unfolding of a miracle. Let us not place limits on God concerning whom He chooses to use, and His methods of unfolding the miracles in our lives.

As humans, the ones with the answers, we are prone to judge and cast judgment based on our experiences - - experiences we deem noteworthy. We are quick to categorize people and place restrictions on them based on age, culture, education, religious persuasion and even gender. God's ways are not our ways, as you have already read in chapter three. We serve a God who is not limited by time and space, as we are; a God who is not boxed in by five senses, emotions and physical limitations. The God who spoke this universe into existence is the God I serve. If He could protect a baby from a harsh king who wanted death for a child, I know He is able to keep me and to keep my children.

I also know He is able to keep you and your family, if you ask Him. I know He will provide for you according to His riches in glory. Take the time to encourage yourself in the Lord as you stop and think of His many blessings to you. You may expect the blessing or protection to come from the east, but He sends it from the west. You think an apnea monitor will alert you, instead He alerts a child. You look to your supervisor for the answer, but the custodian is the one with the "Thus says the Lord." Perhaps you thought the financial blessing would come from your family, but God sent your ethnically different neighbor with the exact amount you needed. You anticipate your answer to come at nine months, but He sends it in the sixth month. What if your miracle was packaged in someone with a different denominational persuasion?

Would you listen?

Would you heed?

Would you accept?

If my parents did not adhere to the voice of a doctor who was used of God, I would not be penning this memoir. I would not be the wife of Roderick, or the mother of four lovely children. Look to the Lord for your future, do not look to your rationale, it can disappoint you and shift your mind away from God.

Beverly Morrison Caesar

Chapter Eleven

HOME TO STAY!

The three-year journey we encountered was like a roller coaster. Nurses came in and out- -twelve hours per day. The trachea tube had to be changed periodically. He was not comfortable with anyone going near his lifeline - - not even for suctioning. It had to grow on him, as he developed a trust for the nurses and even for his parents.

To make Rod comfortable with the changing process, a nurse came up with a brilliant idea. Rod had received an Ernie doll for a Christmas gift -- the Sesame Street, Ernie. He became quite attached to the doll, as the PBS program became one of his favorites. This nurse, Lois, took the time to demonstrate to Rod how similar he and Ernie were. She placed a breathing tube in Ernie's neck, tied it in place and gave the doll to Rod. As he looked at himself in the mirror holding the doll, a common bond was embraced. Each time we had to change his tube, Ernie's tube was changed as well. From that moment on, the procedure never became a challenge for the nurses or for me. The doll became his favorite companion and went everywhere with him. Even during Rod's bath time, Ernie sat and watched from a dry spot!

Emergency trips to the hospital kept our adrenaline on a constant high. He fought fevers, colds, pneumonia and infections. During the fall of his first year home, we were sitting for our annual Christmas family portrait. Our photographer, Charles Gill Sr. , was gracious enough to schedule the sitting at home. By this time Rod was weighing close to eight pounds and was still considered critical. I noticed that he was not as cheerful, jovial or active as he usually was. This gentle, accommodating photographer did his best to generate a smile from Rod - - but without success. Charles suggested continuing the sitting with him asleep instead of trying to reschedule another visit. The important thing was to capture the moment. Rod stayed asleep for the entire shoot - not affording us any photos with his eyes open. Non-the-less, the photos were masterfully executed and our friends, family and church family relished the photos. While we were engrossed in this annual project, a dear friend of ours dropped in for a visit- - she happened to be a medical doctor. Her initial observation was one of concern. Immediately after our project, upon her suggestion, we rushed him to the hospital.

The doctors were on hand as we arrived. He was feverish and had developed pneumonia. For one week he fought the infection, and what a fight that was! His body, tiny for his age, struggled to ward off the infection. He suffered some weight loss, but finally the infection was abated and we brought him home, on medication. This is just one example of the many emergency trips we took back and forth to the hospital.

Rod matured rapidly and had a strong desire for life. As he got older, his physical therapist became a weekly part of his routine. She pulled at him, tugged at him, stretched him and played with him. He was given exercises that I thought were too rigorous for such a small child, but he endured every one of them. The occupational therapist had her chance to influence him as well. His dexterity at handling his bottle, toys, utensils and even crayons was put to the test. He was rewarded each time he successfully accomplished a task. What a joy it was to watch his exuberance when he correctly used his eating utensils, or put the right shoe on the correct foot. Eventually a teacher was added to his already tight schedule. This was great for Rod, as he learned quickly. The relationship between Rod and Mike was unique. It was as if Mike knew Rod before he was born. His skill at communicating with the child was phenomenal. It was as if Rod knew what day of the week Mike was scheduled and the exact time of day. It was amazing. When Mike arrived, Rod would call out his name clearly. He wasn't supposed to be able to push out enough air around his voice box, up through the tube, to speak so clearly. Additionally, a big smile would light up his dimpled face. Mike and the nurses were impressed.

The doctors had informed us that he would not speak until he was seven years old, based on statistics. A speech therapist was sent in to assist in his speech development and again, he amazed everyone. His progress, development and growth rapidly increased above and beyond what was expected. Each pediatric visit was encouraging. His appetite, weight, height, hearing, and vision were exceptional. Every six months at the hospital, Dr. Burke performed a bronchoscopy - - an examination that allows the doctor to see inside the airway. Using laser, the doctor checked to see if his airway widened enough to decanalate him (remove the breathing tube). Blood work had to be done before each visit, and his inaudible cries as the needle entered his arm would break my heart. Each time we went for this ambulatory procedure, I hoped for a miracle. I prayed that he would come home without the tube. But it wasn't God's timing. It was a very uncomfortable time for Rod, as his airway was "poked" into, causing discomfort, swelling, and scar tissue. After each visit, we had to tenderly nurse him back to his normal self. The nurses were familiar with the procedure; therefore they took extra care to address his cries.

Whenever Rod cried, the sound was very faint. If I was in my room and he was crying, I could not hear him at all. One night, after weeks of long days and sleepless nights, I heard his faint cry. My body was tired, my mind needed rest and my patience was fragile. From the day Rod came home, it was a constant ongoing struggle. Sure I had help, but the burden of the load rested on my shoulders. I reached a point where my body was yelling out for rest. On this night in particular, I retired to bed with every intention of awakening to suction Rod at the regular time. I set the alarm, and fell off into a deep sleep. The alarm clock sounded and in my stupor I shut if off and rolled over. Four hours later, a *faint cry* exploded in my ear gate. I jumped up with fear pounding in my chest - - it was Rod! He was in distress! I Rushed into his room. He was struggling to breathe! I awakened Roderick and we immediately began the process. Suctioning was a lost cause - - the mucus had hardened in the tube! Saline solution would take too long to break up the mucus. The only course of action was to take out the tube and replace it with the emergency one. We placed him on the changing table. Roderick tried to keep him still and positioned so that I could cut off the old tube without hurting him. I did this quickly, slid it out of the hole and immediately replaced it with the new tube, tied it in place and added moisture to the area. He was breathing with ease, thank God! Throughout the entire process, we were praying.

We called the doctor and were assured that because he was breathing during the entire process, he was okay. If we noticed anything unusual, then we were to bring him to the emergency room. Everything remained normal. The next morning, the scheduled nurse confirmed his status and congratulated us on our quick action. I am so glad we serve a God who never sleeps or slumbers. Our God is watching us all the time! The Psalmist declares in Psalm 74:16, "The day is His and the night also belongs to Him." Who would not want to serve an Almighty like that? While I was asleep - - in a very deep sleep, He awakened me to the faint cry of my son in distress. I should never have heard that sound - - but God was awake.

Rod's first visit to church was an occasion worth mentioning. This visit was also his official dedication to the Lord. His grandfather, Roderick, Sr. , offered the prayer as he laid his hands on his one and only grandson. It was a joyous celebration as our extended family rejoiced with us. My younger sister, Maxine, and her family joined in the festivities, as his cousins were able to see him for the first time. The grandparents were also on hand for the merrymaking. The Bethel church family rejoiced with us on that glorious Sunday morning when we gave him back to the Lord. They saw first-hand the miracle for which they had been praying. The church family on a whole experienced a growth in faith that extended into their personal lives as well. Testimonies began pouring in of how Rod's miracle served to encourage other mothers who were faced with similar situations. Women began calling me who had challenges with their pregnancies and they simply wanted prayer. I spoke to some women who were considering abortions and told them about the miracle that was unfolding in their bodies. One young girl was one week away from her scheduled abortion, but thank God, the Holy Spirit, through my instructions, altered her plans. Other women reached out to me whose babies were born prematurely, and the babies were experiencing difficulties. I was able to offer hope to these women because I could empathize with them. God gets all the glory for every opportunity I was given to pray with women and offer them hope through the power of God. By His grace I intend to share this testimony to anyone who will listen.

Dr. Henderson, my doctor, called regularly to check on Rod. He had become very interested in his progress. For him, this boy was a true miracle. When Rod began to walk, Dr. Henderson asked us to bring him in for a visit. This would be his first time seeing our son since he delivered him eighteen months earlier. Roderick and I were excited about the visit because we had told Dr. Henderson that God would be the one to keep him alive. He knew we were born-again

Christians, but being a religious Jew, he was simply polite and respected our faith, as we did his.

The glow in his eyes sparkled like light bouncing off a glass spectrum. He picked up Rod, looked at him as if he had never seen anything like it before. He had delivered thousands of babies, alive and well, stillborn, aborted and ill. He had seen two parents who trusted God's Word, not the words of a doctor's medical opinion. Today, he was holding a miracle. I am sure his mind went back to the delivery room when he, through medical eyes, saw what he considered hopeless. And now, to look at, hold, and observe the child he considered not viable at birth, had to impact him tremendously.

He put Rod down and watched him walk around his office, touching, reaching and pulling at everything. Several times I tried to keep Rod still, but each time the doctor's response was, "Leave him alone. If he wants to tear up this office, just let him!"

We enjoyed the visit as much as Dr. Henderson did. Before leaving his office the doctor said, "I'm glad God heard your prayers and not mine."

"You were praying for our son?" I asked him.

"Absolutely yes!" was his convincing response. "But I asked God to take his life."

"Why would you pray such a negative prayer?" Roderick asked, as I picked up Rod and placed him on my lap.

"Well, my concern for the both of you was paramount. I did not want you to have to care for a child who would be a constant burden to you for the rest of your lives. I knew that if he lived, he would definitely require one hundred percent attention the rest of his life. I saw cerebral palsy, blindness, epilepsy, and mental and emotional challenges. I saw you two lovely people with a life-long problem - - that, I didn't want for you. You see, I have a mentally challenged son - - my only son. He is now in his thirties, but he has the capacity of an eight year old. That I did not want for you. I know what my wife and I endured. So, I prayed, and I knew God would understand my heart. He would not bring such a dilemma on two people who were serving Him. I really thought he would hear my prayer, but after the miracle I see today, I'm glad He listened to you." His passion, love and honesty made me respect him even more.

That testimony encouraged me tremendously. Roderick took the time to share some more with Dr. Henderson about our faith in God, His promise to us, and a church that was enveloped in praying for the full recovery of our son. We left that office overjoyed and on cloud nine. Dr. Henderson remains in our lives to this day. He visited Bethel when Roderick was consecrated to the Bishopric, and when I was ordained to the ministry. He expressed that each visit blessed him in an unusual way.

Whenever he visited, the first person he asked for was Rod, and each time the reunion was special.

Leaving the house with our son required careful planning and precise packing. Naomi and Lydia took turns with making sure all his necessary accouterments were included in the travel bag. Of course, all the normal obvious items, such as food and diapers were packed, but additionally, we had to include, suction catheters, packets of saline solution, the emergency trachea tube and the ambu bag. Because we did not travel with the nebulizer machine, we placed a special cover over the trachea tube (see photo on page 81) to allow clean, filtered air to flow into his lungs. It was cumbersome looking, but it was quite effective. On long trips we traveled with *everything,* including the oxygen tank. We would have to call the hotels ahead of time and inform them of our medical needs, and they made certain that all the necessary accommodations were given to us without any difficulty.

The recommendation was made to us that we should enroll Rod in a specialized school that catered to children with speech difficulties. We set up an appointment with a local school in a neighboring community and walked in with Rod for the interview. The idea was to get him prepared so that when he reached three years old, he could begin the preschool program with this special school. The intention was to keep him socially and scholastically on par so that when he became decannelated at seven, he would not be too far behind. The interview began quite normally until they heard Rod speak around the tube.

"How long has he been doing that?" Asked the woman with surprise in her voice.

"For quite some time now," was my response. "We really did not pay that much attention, because it became very normal for us to hear him around the tube."

"Well, this we did not expect. Excuse me for a moment. I'll be right back with my supervisor." Rod, in the meantime, had found a football in the room and was throwing it back and forth to me. The woman came back into the room with her supervisor. They wanted to observe him interacting with me in an observation room. Rod and I were situated so that we were alone. I was to invoke as much conversation with him in this colorful, toy filled room. We had fun together and sure enough he vocalized, not with a loud voice, but audibly guttural so that those watching could not only see him, but also hear him. Eventually they tested his motor skills - - which he passed with no problem. Then they checked his cognitive skills and were impressed with his dexterity at matching, color recognition, size coordination, sequencing and memory. During each test I thanked God for what He was doing for our son. The conclusion was reached that he was too advanced for their program, and we would not be in need of their facility. From every indication they observed, they felt his decanalation would come long before he was seven. What a blessing that was to us! This we had believed and God was beginning to unfold the promise before our very eyes.

God continued showing us miracles morning by morning. I remember during his stay in the hospital and even after he came home, that I would hum the words to a favorite hymn of mine, *Great is Thy Faithfulness*. The exact lyrics that encouraged me were, "Morning by morning new mercies I see, all I have needed thy hands have provided, great is thy faithfulness, Lord, unto me." Each day as I visited my son in the hospital, I looked for new mercies and I was never disappointed. Some mercies were tiny, others were mammoth in proportion, but they were all received with a grateful heart. I believe that those words were penned especially for me. They ministered to me on a daily basis and even today, whenever I hear that hymn, I bless the Lord for all His many mercies, goodness and bountiful benefits toward me and toward my family.

One Thursday night while Roderick was conducting Bible Study at church, an incident took place that called for my immediate attention. The children were asleep and I was quietly putting away the laundry. I had every intention of retiring early. I looked in on the kids, slid into my nightgown and was bedded down for the night. It was almost 10:00 p. m. , so I knew Roderick would be home within the hour. I decided to take one last look at Rod. What I saw caused me to take a double look! I went closer to the crib and looked again. His breathing tube was completely out of his neck and lying to the side, still attached around the neck! *This could not be! How could he be fast asleep so peacefully without the tube in his neck!?* I looked at him again, passed my hand over his face, to see if he would stir, checked to see if his heart was beating and realized that all was well!

I reached for the emergency tube and attempted to put it into his neck, but the opening had closed up! I picked up the phone and dialed my sister's number.

"Call EMS immediately, Beverly!" Sandra cried into the earpiece - - almost deafening my eardrums.

"But he is sleeping so, peacefully. Could this be it? Could he be mature enough to breathe on his own?" I quietly asked this nurse who only thinks with a medical brain.

"No, this is not a miracle. Call EMS and have them come and assess the boy. Don't waste any time, Beverly," came her stern advice. I hung up the phone and called the church. Roderick was leaving, but they caught him just in time. I told him what was happening and he rushed home.

Somehow I was not concerned or alarmed. There was a sweet peace in my spirit as well as in the house. I called EMS. The police always arrived ahead of the Medical Service, with their walkie-talkies blaring. Roderick arrived at the same time and they entered the room with so much commotion that Rod began to stir. He seemed okay, looked at me and began to fret. The commotion is what alarmed him, not his discomfort. I tried to put the tube back into his neck, but to no avail. When EMS arrived, they also attempted - - with no success. They were able to gently force a catheter into the hole, and place an oxygen mask over his nose. To the emergency room again and with police escort. Roderick followed the police in his car while I drove in the EMS vehicle with Rod. He was coping quite well and did not appear to be in any distress. The hospital was awaiting his arrival and immediately attempted to reinsert the tube. No one was successful.

Finally a neonatal doctor was called who was familiar with Rod's case. "Hey, Rod! How ya doing, big boy?" roared this affectionate doctor. After a routine examination, the doctor concluded, "No, Rod could not manage without the trachea tube, he had simply outgrown the size and needed to upgrade to a larger one." *No problem. How do you get the new, larger tube into his neck?* Everyone was watching. Two nurses, an intern, the pediatrician, Roderick and I. After assembling the tube with string in place, the doctor with great force, plunged the tube back into his neck. Blood spewed everywhere and I watched my son writhe in pain as this device was placed back in position. "It looks worse than it really is," said the doctor.

"The skin had hardened just a little and only needed enough pressure to pry it open. If you had waited a day or two, then we would have had to go another way, but these few hours were not critical." Although the explanation was believable, I could not help but cry along with my son. I felt the pain as much as he did. He stayed overnight for observation, and by noon the next day he was home with a larger tube in place.

Chapter Twelve

WHAT? . . . AGAIN?!

Life for the family was progressing at a comfortable pace. Rod was improving at record speed and the girls were not only enjoying their baby brother, but they were also excelling in school. Roderick's missionary ventures were taking him to India, Africa and the West Indies. Bethel was expanding and the ministry flourishing. I was lending leadership to the women's ministry, the fundraising program and the publications department. I had reached a comfort zone in my life. Comfortable with ministry, comfortable with the family, comfortable with my relationship with Roderick, and I was not looking for anything to rock the boat. I absolutely had no plans for another child, not in this life! *Oh, No! Look somewhere else. Find another carrier, not this one. My quiver is more than full.* My mind was fixed on that thought; therefore, when I missed my cycle, I was in no way alarmed. When the second month rolled around and I still had not seen my period, denial set in. *This is just early menopause,* I mused to myself. *Some women begin the change of life process in their late thirties, early forties* came my rationale. *God would never do this to me - - not after all my body has been through. He loves me too much.* The reasoning continued for another two weeks. I had all the signs of being pregnant, but I ignored them all! *I could not be! It can't be!* I brooded, whined, complained and criticized. I even hoped for a miscarriage. I determined in my mind that I would not see my doctor. I would just let nature take its course. I was certain that if I did nothing, based on past experiences, I would definitely lose the baby; it was settled!

So many things were going on in my mind. I remembered Robyn's words to me concerning another pregnancy, and I certainly hoped to prove her wrong. Another child would upset the perfect family set up - - we had no more room in the house. The girls shared a room and Rod was comfortable in his room.

Where would we put another child?

What would people say?

What would they think?

What about my health?

God, how could you do this to me?

I functioned in a state of despair.

I was not emotionally ready to deal with another child. What overwhelmed me the most was the confinement that faced me, the uncertainty of the pregnancy, my age, and, my well - being. Roderick and I discussed what was unfolding, and as usual he was wise in his counsel. "You had better pull yourself together and stop brooding and feeling sorry for yourself. If you are really pregnant your attitude will adversely affect the child. I suggest you call the doctor, get the prenatal care you need, and let's move on." I know his rebuke was from a loving heart. He was right! I just did not want to hear it. I wanted sympathy. I wanted a shoulder to cry on.

I braced myself, took his counsel and called the doctor. Not only was Dr. Henderson on vacation, but he no longer practiced

Obstetrics. We decided to find another doctor who specialized in crisis pregnancies and ended up with Dr. Bender. Roderick and I walked into the office and waited to be called. This was all too familiar. All I could think about, as I looked around at the eager young couples, was that I wished I were somewhere else. *I am too old for this - - I am almost forty.* We went into Dr. Bender's office and a complete history of my medical journey was taken. He began to give his opinion. Based upon my chronicle, his thought was that I had what is called an incompetent cervix. If upon examination, I was indeed pregnant, he would have to perform a cerclage - - sewing the cervix closed. He indicated that my cervix dilated in the fifth month causing the fetus to go into the delivery mode - - hence the miscarriages. Fibroids only helped to complicate matters, but the cervix was the true culprit.

He discussed amniocentesis because of my age, and strongly recommended that I have the procedure done. After much prayer and counseling, we opted not to do the procedure. We concluded that whatever the findings were, we were going to have the child, and that was our personal conviction. However, if you are faced with this option, please consider the counsel of your doctor, the counsel of the Lord, and your own personal convictions.

As I entered the examination room, I began to feel a deep sense of guilt. Here I was already twelve weeks into the pregnancy, knowing what the ramifications could be without prenatal care. I tried to shake the feeling, but the culpability overpowered me. As the doctor placed the heartbeat monitor over my abdomen and began listening to the baby's - - what I heard made me weep. I had heard that sound so many times before and had never wept. This time, guilt, shame, dishonor, and condemnation gripped my heart. I cried uncontrollably. The doctor asked if I was okay. I assured him that I was, but that I needed some time to myself. He completed the examination and left the room. The heartbeat - - lup dup, lup dup, lup-dup rang over and over in my ear. A child was growing and living inside me, and I had taken this miracle for granted.

I Cried. God, God, Oh God, I cried, *Please, please forgive me. I'm so sorry for the way I've behaved. After all the miracles you have done for me, please forgive me.* I felt guilty for God even giving Rod to me. The tears were unending. *What if something is wrong with the baby?* I began to blame myself for anything that could go wrong because of my delay in seeing the doctor. Concern was momentarily replaced with guilt.

I slowly dressed, and meditatively left the room with a feeling of melancholy in my belly that I'll never forget. *So many women are unable to have children, and here I am carrying a life and regretting it. How can I be so ungrateful to God?* I felt like shouting from the rooftop to anyone in the sound of my voice of how foolish I'd been. I was impressed with a strong compulsion right then and there that I had to share this experience with everyone. Why? To show how ungrateful we sometimes are as people. We take a lot for granted. God wanted me to declare that we cannot put our confidence in this flesh; it will fail us every time. Remember, honesty is the only road that will lead to peace of mind. Hiding an illness can eventually lead to death. Denying the existence of a growing fetus, for me, was unconscionable after the miracles God unfolded in my life.

Not admitting one's flaws will lead to deception, compromise and ultimate failure. I knew I had to convey a message of how forgetful we can be of God's many benefits toward us. I had to remind those who would listen, that this selfish nature has to be crucified daily. I had taken for granted what many women had hoped and prayed for. I had failed God in stewardship of the blessings He bestowed upon me. How could I, of all people, not trust the Lord? The Lord had proven to me that his love was unconditional. I had failed Him - - yet He blessed me with a son. I had disappointed Him, yet He unfolded a miracle before my very eyes. El-Shaddai, the Almighty, had proven to me that nothing was too hard for Him, as He had proven to Sarah and Abraham (Genesis 18:14). I learned first-hand that all power is copiously expressed in the term God or EL. He is the Mighty One who nourishes, provides and satisfies. Sure, I had heard that before, but now I knew it for myself. I embraced the fact that I served the Almighty, El-Shaddai who pours out blessings, favors, and sustenance upon mankind, upon undeserving me! "It is God as El who helps, but it is God as Shaddai who abundantly blesses with all manner of blessings," states Nathan Stone in his book, **Names Of God** (Moody Press, Chicago, 1944 p. 34). God helped me to understand his workings and Shaddai poured out His abundant blessings upon me. What a glorious thing! He had taken my hands and walked with me through some difficult valleys and even poured out blessings as He had done with the Shunammite woman (2 Kings 4).

The Lord also wanted me to tell anyone who would listen that His power to forgive is instantaneous. What I was experiencing, He had already dealt with on Calvary - - the burden of shame, guilt and condemnation. It was now up to me to receive His forgiveness, and leave the burdens at the cross. He prompted me to change my negative attitude, put on the garment of praise and speak life into the child I was carrying. "Death and life are in the power of the tongue," Proverbs 18:21. "From the heart the mouth speaks," Luke 6:45. Those scriptures popped into my spirit as I continued to pray.

As I cried and prayed, I began to accept His forgiveness, and I could move on from the seat of this staggering guilt. God forgives us immediately when we pray from a penitent heart. The most difficult part is for us to forgive ourselves. That was where I found myself that Saturday afternoon in the doctor's office. I had accepted God's forgiveness, and began the work of forgiving myself. It did not take long at all.

I assured the doctor that my tears were personal and confirmed to him that I was all right. He shared with us in consultation, that what he saw during the examination was what he had suspected. A date was scheduled for the cerclage, and I headed for the hospital one more time. Under anesthesia, the procedure was completed and three days later I was sent home with several restrictions. Lovemaking was limited - - Roderick had to be patient and considerate. I was limited to the house. Yes, I could venture outside, but with caution.

A machine that monitored contractions and movements was placed in the house. Once-per-day for one hour, I would do a *sitting*. I would strap the monitoring belt around my abdomen, turn on the machine and any contractions would be transmitted to a main computer at the hospital. This would alert the technicians of any unusual movement, sound, contractions and the doctor would be immediately informed. If at any time outside the scheduled *sitting* time, I felt any unusual pain or sensations, I would call the main office and alert them that I would be doing a *sitting*. They would immediately begin processing the reading on their end. The cost of the machine was astronomical, but I thank God for good insurance. On two occasions, the contractions were cause for alarm, but bed rest solved those concerns.

Four months into the pregnancy I developed full-blown gestational diabetes. I was back into the hospital for one week. It was difficult leaving Rod at home for such a long time. Roderick brought him to the hospital, but I could only wave to him from my window. The main purpose for the hospitalization was to try and control the diabetes through diet. After the third day, the conclusion was reached that I had to be placed on insulin. At that point in my pregnancy, the baby's pancreas was trying to do the work for the both of us. That would not do.

I had watched my father for years administer his own insulin, but I never dreamed that one day I would have to do the same. My previous gestational diabetes had been controlled through diet, but not this one. After much trepidation, I resigned myself to this task and began learning how to apply the insulin myself - - finding an arm, leg, thigh, or stomach muscle and injecting the insulin into that muscle. This I had to do three-times-per-day. Also, I had to administer finger sticks six times daily to be certain the blood sugar levels were just right - - never below 55- and never above 115 for my personalized case. I had to keep an accurate recording because the personalized unit I had was hooked up to the hospital's computer system, enabling them to download all my entries for assessment. During my prenatal visit all the readings were assessed.

Having to concentrate on this added scenario to my life made my motherly duties challenging. Mommy came to live with us for a while. She took up where the nurses left off with Rod and also helped with Naomi and Lydia. Our housekeeper was still on hand to keep the house in order. Roderick's ministry at Bethel was curtailed, but he still had his hands full.

During my pregnancy, Rod did not experience any emergencies that kept him in the hospital - -thank God! I still was able to keep up with his development, the girls, my personal medical needs and to spend time with Roderick. It was very difficult, but God brought us through. He was faithful to us!

I felt a level of unhappiness for my husband, though, as he had to deal with so much unfolding in our lives. We could not be as intimate as we would have liked and, this bothered me. By nature, Roderick is a passionate and affectionate man. He is the hugging, kissing, touching type. For a good portion of our marriage he had to deal with not having, on a regular basis, the intimate expressions husbands and wives are known to enjoy. He had to deal with two miscarriages - - one with me on full bed rest, and two pregnancies where bed rest was the only option. As I write this memoir, I dedicate this chapter to men who tenderly and graciously accommodate their wives in the challenging situations of life.

Your experience may be very different from ours, but I am sure the challenges are similar. Your wife may have had to deal with a severe illness or a situation(s) that left her totally dependent upon you. She may have been in a coma, had to deal with chemotherapy, radiation or even amputation of a limb. Perhaps blindness came knocking on her door, or crippling multiple sclerosis or early Alzheimer's. Only eternity will tell the rewards you will earn for "hanging in there." Your faithfulness to her will be manifested as a jewel in your crown. The end product of your patience and diligence, I am sure, will be worth the sacrifice.

The Bible encourages us not to become weary in doing well - - in doing the right thing (Galatians. 6:9). If we hold on, He assures us that in due season (in HIS time) we will reap (gain our rewards) if we do not faint. So, men of God, men of faith and men of courage, hold on to the promises found in God's Word. May God bless your life as you have blessed the life of your wife. May your children and children's children rise up and give you double the honor that is due to you. As you have honored your wife, and loved her, may other men look to you as an example of integrity in action. May the riches of heaven be yours because of your labor of love - - doing well on behalf of your wife.

If, for whatever reason, you were unable to stand up under the load, the forgiving God is on your side; condemnation is not aimed your way. God's grace and mercy are flowing in your direction. Repentance is a personal issue and that is what God is looking for. When repentance is genuine, God removes the transgressions from us forever. (Psalm 103:12)

JULY 2008

THURSDAY 3

My Prayer

I ask for strength
and God gave me
difficulties to make me
strong.

FRIDAY 4

Independence Day (US)

I ask for wisdom
and God gave me problems
to learn to solve!

SATURDAY 5

I ask for prosperity
and God gave me brain &
brawn to work.

SUNDAY 6

I ask for courage and
He gave me troubled
people to help.

next side →

AT-A-GLANCE ®

JUNE						
S	M	T	W	T	F	S
1	2	3	4	5	6	7
8	9	10	11	12	13	14
15	16	17	18	19	20	21
22	23	24	25	26	27	28
29	30					

JULY						
S	M	T	W	T	F	S
		1	2	3	4	5
6	7	8	9	10	11	12
13	14	15	16	17	18	19
20	21	22	23	24	25	26
27	28	29	30	31		

AUGUST						
S	M	T	W	T	F	S
					1	2
3	4	5	6	7	8	9
10	11	12	13	14	15	16
17	18	19	20	21	22	23
24	25	26	27	28	29	30
31						

JULY 2008

7 MONDAY

I ask for favours and
God gave me oppurtunities.

I received nothing I
wanted.

8 TUESDAY

I received everything I
needed.
My prayer has been answered

Done by: Amariah Carla Burton

9 WEDNESDAY

As God's love is unconditional, that is all I have to extend to you as well. Walk in forgiveness and may you use the rest of your years ahead to love your wife and glorify God. When God becomes the focal point of your life, loving your wife and others will become second nature.

Ephesians 4:25 tells the husband to love his wife as Christ loved the church and gave Himself for it. This is a tall order, but not an impossibility. God can give you that kind of love for your wife which will not only please Him, but will give you benefits beyond measure. Cherish this special gift God has given to you, and with the Lord's help, don't look back with reproach. Use your experience to minister to others. You may have lost some precious years that cannot be redeemed, but do not focus on what you did, or what you did not do, but do the best with what you have NOW. As one flesh - - husband and wife - - I pray that you will value each one above the other, as you put God first in your lives.

Chapter Thirteen

VICTORY

With Rod's "big boy" tube in place, his development seemed to take off. He had two more bronchoscopies and after the third attempt, the doctor was very hopeful with his progress. His airway looked good! It appeared that he could finally manage on his own.

Entering his third year, exactly one month and one day before his birthday, on April 3rd, 1992, with progress on our side, and hope in our hearts, we took the trip to the hospital. His nurse, Lois, was on hand for the trek; Grandma Myrtle, Naomi, Lydia, Roderick and I looked forward with excitement to the experience. Rod held on to Ernie as we explained to him that both of them were having their trachea tubes removed. It was a simple, uneventful procedure.

After a routine examination by a nurse - - blood pressure, temperature, weight, and a treatment of Proventil, Dr. Burke walked into the room and greeted us. The doctor smiled and said to Rod, "Today is your big day, are you ready? I think Ernie is all ready." Rod smiled and glanced at Ernie. The doctor assured Rod that he had nothing to fear, as he was about to go near his trachea tube. He carefully cut the string that held the tube in place and gently slid the tube out of his neck. He then placed a gauze strip over the opening and gave us a "thumbs up!" Dr. Burke gave me the tube to keep as a memento. The nurse untied Ernie's tube and placed it in Rod's hands, and that was it! In a few days the hole would close, and the only indication of any kind would be a permanent scarring on his neck.

Victory!

Sieg!

Victoria!

PaBYEda!

Victoire!

Mmeri!

The scar on his neck serves as a constant reminder of the faithfulness of God to us. For us, it is a memorial to God of His keeping power and His miraculous intervention. Rod does not have any noticeable indication of being a preemie, as is common in most preemies. I believe that God left us the scar so we would never forget the miracle He unfolded in our lives. We stayed on the hospital grounds for the rest of the day for observations. Rod acted as if nothing had changed. Here I was, amazed at the sudden finality of the decanalation. I watched him closely, looking for anything abnormal - - nothing! He was just as active, playful, talkative and happy as before. I shook my head in awe at how simple and uneventful things had turned out. The doctor warned us that he would, for the first few years after the decannalation, suffer from upper respiratory distress, especially in the winter. If we kept a close watch on him, there should be no cause for alarm. We headed home.

Four months later, I was taken to the hospital to give birth through, Caesarean section to a nine-pound baby girl. Her sugar levels were a cause for concern, so she stayed in the intensive care unit for ten days. Thank God she was diabetes free, healthy and normal, and so was I. Bringing her home was another time for rejoicing. I call her "God's little extra," Elizabeth Gabrielle Caesar. I wanted to abort another miracle, but God, the life giver, had the better plan. "Lo, children are a heritage of the Lord and the fruit of the womb is His reward" Psalm 127:3. When I finally got the chance to be alone, I thanked God for the four miracles He allowed to come my way.

As I reminisce, my state of mind and mental condition were no better than the intentions and plans of my parents. Their decision to abort the miracle was borne out of poverty and misguided counsel. My decision to wait for a miscarriage was predicated upon selfishness, forgetfulness and self-pity. God looked beyond our human actions and honored us with miracles. Providence is in the hands of the Sovereign, Almighty, Jehovah Elohim - the Eternal Creator. His purpose for the Morrisons and Caesars went beyond our limited comprehension. Before time, God knew that a man named Roderick Richardson Caesar, Sr. , would honor Him with a life and ministry of integrity. He also knew ahead of time, that this heritage should live on, not only through his son, Roderick Jr. but also through his grandson, Roderick, III. God also brought a young woman who was given a chance of life, from Jamaica, West Indies to America; a young woman whose parents heeded the voice of an abortion doctor and saved their daughter, Beverly, from being a statistic. God providentially brought Roderick and Beverly together, to fulfill His divine purpose not only for a family, but also for a ministry. Because Hector and Veronica obeyed God, I am able to share and appreciate this wonderful miracle of life!

When I accepted the call of God on my life in 1995, my mom paid me a visit. She sat down with me and shared her miraculous testimony. I remembered asking her why she never told it to me before.

"I was ashamed and embarrassed. What I intended to do was not something you boast about, or even talk about," said Mommy.

"But you could have told me. I was the one you were considering to abort. That information would have helped me a long time ago," came my response.

"When you told me that you were going into ministry full-time as an ordained minister, I knew it was time to share the testimony with you. I always knew that God had His hand on your life from the time you were born. I didn't know what He was going to do with your life, but I knew you were different. When you married Roderick, I thought that was it. When Rod III was born, I thought to myself, that was it. Even when little Elizabeth came on the scene, I knew that was the reason God kept you here. But when you accepted the ministerial call of God on your life, I was certain this was the most pivotal reason for your life. I knew I had to tell you. My dear, everything that has come your way, from your marriage, to your children, to your ministry, are all ordained and destined of God. I had nothing to do with it." Mommy concluded with tears in her eyes.

"Oh yes you did! You could have gone on with your plans and found another doctor to complete your intentions, but you were sensitive to God," was my choked-up response.

"God was and is still in control of your life no matter what else comes your way. You had to bring in the next generation to take Bethel to a new level," Mommy continued, barely above a whisper.

I began to cry as I considered that Mommy did truthfully have an option. It brought to mind one of my favorite Christmas movies, *It's A Wonderful Life*, starring James Stewart. The plot of the movie is about a man living in a small town with nothing going for him - - so he thought. Life was not unfolding the way he had hoped, and so he wanted to end it. An angel interrupted his attempted suicide and took him on a journey to show him what his town and the world would have been like without him. At the conclusion of the angel's visit, this man was able to realize how valuable he was to hundreds of people. He prayed and asked God to give him another chance at life. Although this is a secular movie, the moral of the plot is one from which we can gain insight. Life is precious, valuable and no life is an accident. I give God thanks for Mommy and Daddy who gave me a chance at life.

God has a wonderful PLAN for your life. Salvation is a planned gift from God, and if you have not received this gift, I invite you to reach out and take it. God loved you so much that He sent His only Son, Jesus, to die on a cruel cross for you. A cross that had your name on it; all because you were born in sin. But God's love looked beyond your natural sinful state and planned the gift of salvation just for you. It is quite simple. The Bible states in Romans 6:23, "For the wages of sin is death; but the gift of God is eternal life through Jesus Christ our Lord." The Bible further indicates that, "If we confess our sins, he is faithful and just to forgive us our sins and to cleanse us from all unrighteousness." 1 John 1:9. You cannot buy this salvation. The Lord Jesus already paid the price for you on Calvary. All He asks is that you believe that He is the Son of the Living God, and acknowledge that you are a sinner in need of a Savior. Ask Him to forgive you and cleanse you from all unrighteousness. As you invite the Lord to become your Savior, He receives you with open arms. When you pray that simple prayer of repentance, salvation is yours. It is that simple. God has a PLAN for your life and He wants to fulfill that plan for His glory. Take the plunge. I guarantee you that your life will never be the same, and the peace of God will become a vital part of your life.

If you are walking with the Lord, I challenge you to step out in the PLAN God has for your life. He wants His **Purpose Lived** through you to Affect your Neighbors. He wants you to make a difference in your community by the life you live on a consistent basis. Your experiences in life come so that your testimony will affect the lives of others. Do not minimize how God can use your experiences to bless others and to be a source of encouragement to many. Do not place God in a box because of your shortsightedness. Let Him open to you the windows of heaven and pour our blessings upon you your family, your community and the nation because of your obedience.

Chapter Fourteen

THE SUM OF IT ALL

Abortion, a word that usually refers to the taking of the life of an unborn fetus, rings out consternation to many Christians; not only to Christians, but also to anyone who believes in the divine sanctity of life.

Life is believed to be sacred.

Life is a miracle.

Miracles unfold every day.

God gives life and He is the only one who should take it. Miscarriages, however, are viewed in a different light. They are inevitable courses of events that operate outside of man's control when nature takes an unfortunate turn and a fetus is lost. Although sometimes misunderstood, it is not condemned.

Abortion, when uttered, usually, speaks of one thing and one thing only - - the taking of a life while in the uterus resulting in individuals never given the opportunity to live. Lives taken for many reasons; indiscretion, fear of the future, incest, perplexities of marriage, career goals, rape, youthful lusts, and even misguided advice. Human beings not granted one moment in time - - their lives snatched from them before they had a chance to utter their first cry.

Lives taken to seemingly save that of the mother. A person destroyed because the life he/she faced would be filled with physical and or mental challenges. Aborted because someone else determined what the outcome should be.

There is another type of abortion that cannot be overlooked, and that is what I call, *purpose abortion.* This refers to anyone who, through various circumstances aborted the plans God had for their lives. Individuals not fulfilling their divine god-given purpose. Individuals living below their destiny because of choices they made. Individuals hurt because they were constantly told that they were nothing and that nothing good could ever become of their lives. Individuals who bought the "lie." Satan's lies! Let me encourage you in this manner. God is a forgiving savior who will forgive sin when repentance is genuine. A repentant heart not only seeks forgiveness, but a repentant heart also desires change.

A turning takes place.

Turning from sin unto righteousness.

Turning from self to God.

A true repentant person recognizes the mistakes, accepts responsibility for sinning and seeks to be forgiven. When this occurs, God's grace begins the process of forgiving. God hears and sees the heart of the individual and restoration takes place. So, if you are genuinely sorry for committing the act of abortion, whether physical abortion or missing your life's purpose, God has erased the act, and you can begin with a new slate. He grants the opportunity to begin anew, as if you were born all over again! He can also remove the guilt and the shame of your actions, if you allow Him to. The most difficult part of receiving forgiveness is forgiving yourself. You hold on to the memory of your actions and even carry around the emotional pain for years. Remember, God forgave you the moment you repented. He threw your sins into the sea of forgetfulness, never to be remembered anymore. Do not allow anyone to remind you of your failures. Do not allow your mind to haunt you of your indiscretions. Do not allow Satan to "throw" into your face what God has already forgiven and what He has covered through the shed blood of His son Christ Jesus. I encourage you to let go of your past mistakes, let go of your past failures, let go of the hurts and the pain and allow the loving God to pour out His tender love into your soul. When you do this, then...

You are free! You are free! You are free!

My birthday always falls on or around Mother's Day weekend, as I was born on May 12th. Every Mother's Day, I take the time to publicly thank God for life. I let Satan know that what he intended for evil, God turned around for His honor and for His glory. As long as God grants me life and health, I will share my testimony to those I meet. I hope that from this testimony a life will be snatched from the plans of abortion. I pray that a challenging pregnancy will end up a miracle for God's glory. I pray that churches, marriages and families will embrace their miracles, embrace their destinies, and hold on to the promises God birthed in their spirits and in their hearts. It is my aim to declare wherever I go that God's plan for a life is precious and it is sacred. The wonderful gifts He has given to us can be realized if we place our trust in Him. I want people to know that the power of God upon a life can abort Satan's plans. God's power can also change the world... through YOU! What if Billy Graham's mother had another plan? What if Ben Carson's mother didn't care? What if Helen Keller's mother gave up hope? Mother Theresa... What if? Harriet Tubman... What if? What about you?

From the day Rod's trachea tube was removed, he was hospitalized four times for short stints. One summer while at our camp in upstate, New York, he suffered a severe upper respiratory attack for which a treatment of Proventil at a local hospital stabilized his breathing.

When Rod was about seven years old, very active, rambunctious and athletic, he experienced a setback. We were in California for a family vacation at the time. I noticed that he was sleeping a lot, that he was listless and lethargic. He had a fever that would not subside. Tylenol and tepid washcloths applied to his forehead would not break the fever. For the first time since his decannelatioin, I noticed that his breathing was extremely labored indenting his chest cavity as he inhaled and exhaled. This attack caused concern to overtake me. Talking was an effort for him and all he wanted to do was to sleep. At about 2:00 a.m. one morning, his breathing was so labored that Roderick and I packed him up and rushed him to a local hospital. In the emergency room we found out that the over-the-counter medicine that I had given to him had worked negatively against him. It had caused his heart rate to speed up, accelerating his breathing, causing great stress on his heart and lungs. They administered the correct dosage of Proventil and he stayed in the hospital for two days. After he stabilized, we were able to continue our vacation without incident. Thank God for His intervening grace and mercy.

LAST WORDS

To date of the memoir, Rod is not asthmatic, nor sickly. Roderick Richardson Caesar, III, currently at sixteen years of age is home schooled and is in the tenth grade. Reading is one of his passions. He is a normal teenager, with acne, who enjoys basketball, tennis, swimming and gymnastics.

He has a lovely singing voice. He sings in the youth choir at Bethel, plays the piano and loves the Lord passionately. His musical repertoire includes singing the baritone solo, *Refiner's Fire* from Handel's Messiah. He also appeared on the *TBN Hudson River Valley Praise The Lord* program singing, *Above All* by Michael W. Smith. He is not only a classical and gospel singer, but he also raps. Roderick ministers with a group of young men and women, sharing the gospel through contemporary music in rap form. This group, "Militant Christians" is passionate about the things of God and their lyrics impress their peers that Jesus in the life makes a difference. They communicate the message effectively as their words are clear, hitting the designated target with God's power.

Rod is also active as a core leader for the Joppa Ministry. This ministry serves to accommodate young people ages 12 through 18. He is maturing nicely as a teenager and he knows that the hand of God is upon his life. His dad and I keep the miracle alive before him, so that he never takes his life for granted. Oh, by the way, the Ernie doll is still in his room!

Elizabeth Gabrielle Caesar, home schooled as well, is in the sevnth grade. She sings in the choir and is learning to play the bassoon. She learned how to crochet at the capable hands of Arlene Boyce and has become quite proficient at it. She also has the call of God on her life and makes no bones about her intentions of being active in ministry in the future. At the tender age of twelve she declares without coercion, "One day I'm going to help my brother pastor Bethel." I call her "God's little extra."

Lydia, our second born, is currently a senior in college, majoring in theater. She is a gifted and talented young woman who zealously loves the Lord and loves her family. She is a dramatist, a singer and a seamstress - in her own right, creating unique accessories. She played the bassoon and the piano, which served to enhance her musical ability. Lydia has an evangelistic calling on her life. She is a born leader. From the day she entered this world with her vibrant, boisterous, cry, I knew God was going to use her to declare His truths.

One of the many lessons I have learned from my experiences is that, Satan will attempt to circumvent the plans of God at any cost. He could not kill nor destroy me, so he went after Lydia.

In August 2003, Lydia shared with us that she was three months pregnant. She and her boyfriend Denarius, sat before us with tears in their eyes expressing their dilemma. Needless to say we were taken aback at the announcement and very disappointed with their conduct. They genuinely repented. Recognizing the errors of their actions, they begged our forgiveness. After the expected scolding, reprimanding, deliberating and venting, we forgave them. Roderick challenged them to seriously consider their actions. He had them promise to honor God in their behavior until the baby was born. In between tears they prayerfully promised to respect each other and to trust God to keep them true to their promise. We in turn, pledged our support and prayed with and for them.

Lydia and I had several personal conversations. I learned from our sharing that she was encouraged by different people to have an abortion.

"Mommy, I realized that the mistake was not that I got pregnant, the mistake was having sex outside of marriage." As she continued speaking, I realized that my little girl had grown up!

"I never expected this to happen to me. You know how I used to talk and I would tell you that I would never embarrass you with a pr-marital pregnancy?"

Sure I remember!

"But, I trusted in ME! I became self-confident, and cocky instead of trusting the Lord." As I listened, the tears came. (By now you know that I am a crybaby). I just allowed her to talk. I was sensing that she wanted to vent.

She continued, "God never makes a mistake - - so I know that the baby is not a mistake. Abortion never crossed my mind - - it was never an option."

"Thank God you didn't go that route. You know better than that."

"Yes, you and daddy instilled godly principles in me and I would never compound my life by adding any more guilt to what I was already dealing with. I disappointed God, I disappointed you, daddy, my church family and I certainly disappointed myself." The tears rolled off her cheeks and I felt her pain. I was too choked up to speak.

"Mommy, I learned how to be strong from watching you. I watched you pull yourself up when things got challenging." Lydia always knew how to express herself.

"Lyd, you know my strength comes from the Lord," I replied, barely above a whisper.

"I know. But I had to lean on what I saw in you to know that I could make it. I'm sorry for not coming to you sooner, but I was so disappointed in myself for hurting you." Her words were punctuated by sniffles - - the tears flowed and she did not try to stop them, neither did I. We just hugged and cried with each other.

Six months later, I was privileged to be in the delivery room, along with Denarius, to hold my daughter's hands as she delivered a healthy baby girl. For me the privilege was two fold: firstly, to witness the birth of my first grandchild, and secondly to witness first hand a vaginal delivery. All my children were born by Caesarean delivery, so, I cherished every moment of watching Kayliah come into the world, on February 24, 2004. But Satan had another tactic up his sleeve.

Three months later on May 11, 2004, I received a phone call from my husband that sent my blood pressure soaring. I had just arrived home after a tiring day at the office. My intentions were to get a load off my feet and relax for a few moments before resuming my schedule.

"Don't be alarmed, but Lydia was in a car accident," I heard Roderick say on the other end of my cell phone. Well, what kind of response should one give when one is told such a thing? I felt an upsurge of dread.

"What?"

"Where?"

"When?"

"How did it happen?"

"Is she okay?"

"Was Kaye with her?"

"I'm my way!" I did not give him a chance to answer any of the questions. I immediately went into a "let me go and save her mode."

"Slow down, slow down, calm down, everything is okay!" Came his 'trying to be calm' voice. I knew better.

"What happened?" I asked, rushing to get out of the house.

"Do not come to the scene of the accident, go straight to Jamaica Hospital, she and Kaye are in the ambulance. They are fine!"

"Fine? How could they be fine in an ambulance?" Was my puzzled response.

"Just trust me. They need you at the hospital. I'll stay here at the scene and make sure everything is okay."

"Roderick, I am NOT going any where until I hear what happened. My heart cannot take this. You are there, you know what happened - - my mind is all over the place. Talk to me." I pleaded with him.

"Promise me you'll go. And I'll talk with you while you are on your way." I promised, but I did not hang up the phone.

Lydia had left the church with Kaye, safely secured in her baby seat. They were on their way to the gas station - - the gas tank was close to being empty. A slight drizzle was refreshing the atmosphere. As Lydia turned unto a main street that led to her destination, her world changed. A young woman coming in the opposite direction from a side street did not see Lydia, because a parked tractor-trailer had blocked her vision. A collision was inevitable! Lydia, in her attempt to steer away from the collision, swerved the car to avoid contact. However, The woman's car hit the Envoy at the back door, clipping the back tire and sending Lydia's car air borne. The car did one complete summersault and landed on its roof. It skidded down the block, crushing metal, shattering glass, collecting debris and strewing the contents of the vehicle all over the street, until it eventually came to a complete stop. Police sirens echoed across the Jamaica community. Fire trucks and emergency vehicles rushed to the scene of the accident.

Lydia recalls the accident in this manner:

"I knew I was going to die. I heard Kayliah screaming - I knew she would be history. As the car skidded down the road, I envisioned debris coming through the windshield and decapitating my head. I closed my eyes and waited for something dreadful to happen. I thought the car would burst into flames. I knew that it was over for me. I was screaming, "Jesus!" "Jesus!" I thought the car would never stop - - then finally it came to a complete halt. I heard someone say, 'Help her out.' I remember yelling. 'My baby, my baby; get her out, get her out!' To my astonishment, someone had already un-strapped the crying child and she was safe in the arms of a stranger. I was assisted out of the car through the driver's window - - with NOT A SCRATCH on my body. How did Kayliah get out so quickly? I believe that for a few moments I must have blacked out after the car came to a complete stop. In my minds eye, I was alert the entire time, therefore I could not have missed them taking Kaye out of the car. Maybe I was in shock and did not realize what was happening around me. Never-the-less, God sent angels to protect me and to protect my three-month-old child from what could have been a fatal car accident. I also know that if my car was full of gasoline, this story would have ended differently. The other driver was repeatedly apologetic as she realized the error was on her part. I am just glad to be alive!"

After being examined by the doctors at the hospital, Lydia and Kayliah were dismissed without any medical challenges whatsoever. God came through for them, in their 25th hour!"

Imagine, one day before my 52nd birthday, Satan tried to abort the lives of two of my generations - - my daughter and my granddaughter. But thanksgiving goes to God who is always on the case. He never sleeps and He never slumbers. He was with my mother 53 years earlier to circumvent an abortion, and He was with Lydia and Kayliah, to prevent the premature snatching of two lives. To God be the glory!

Lydia and Denarius are engaged and will be married in the fall of 2005.

Naomi, a freelance graphic designer is presently working for Bethel in the publications department. A student at Pratt Institute, she is on the path to earning her masters degree in communication design. Naomi is a member of Bethel's worship team. As a vocalist she sings on many fronts. She has ministered in Handel's Messiah and in numerous church productions. She also appeared on the *TBN Hudson River Valley Praise The Lord* program with her father and also with Pastor Jacqueline McCullough.

She currently assists me with dramatic presentations, which demands a lot of her time. Her assistance is vital to the success of the productions. She also recognizes her place in ministry and will eventually join the administrative team in the near future. A prophetic mantel rests on her, and the Lord is presently fine-tuning her gifts.

Naomi has faced her own demons and she could pen a memoir that would encourage pastor's children, and young people who are involved in ministry.

I know that my children are destined for greatness. As they continue to fear the Lord, honor their parents, respect leadership and remain diligent in all their ways, God will grant them the desires of their hearts. He will also honor the prayers of their parents, grandparents, and the prayers of God's people.

My dad, Hector George Morrison, is in heaven and so is my father-in-law, Roderick Richardson Caesar, Sr. I am delighted that both grandfathers had the privilege of being a part of my son's life. I am indebted to God, especially for allowing Rod to know his paternal grandfather before he closed his eyes in death. He lived to the ripe old age of 98 - - what a blessing! Rod was ten years old when he died. Occasionally Rod would lament to me that he wished he had taken the time to learn more from his grandfather. I believe that whatever was poured into Rod through his grandfather will surface when he needs it.

My mother, Veronica Morrison continues to be a source of strength as the matriarch of the Morrison family. She is active in her home church, active in the community and volunteers at a local hospital. Mommy's spiritual gifts flow in the areas of encouragement, word of wisdom and faith. She still finds the time to be a grandmother to her thirteen grandchildren, and is the spiritual stalwart of our family. Her great granddaughter has arrived as an added blessing in her life.

My brother, Dennis, lives in Jamaica, West Indies, with his wife and one of his three daughters. He continues to actively serve the Lord in his local assembly. My sisters, Sandra and Maxine, are also active in their local churches in Pennsylvania and Maryland, respectively. My sister-in-love, Beverly, works along side her brother as one of Bethel's Ministers. Her daughter, Rhonda, is also on staff at Bethel.

Robyn, continues to hear from the Lord and has become a proven prophet for this time. She is currently pastoring with Rev. Jacqueline McCullough, in Pacoma, New York.

My church family endeavors to be a faith - believing ministry with a strong teaching, equipping, empowering and sending focus. I am honored to belong to a family of believers whose eyes are on Christ and not on man. You see, they have seen for themselves that it is the Almighty who is in control, who has chosen to use mortal man to fulfill His plan on the earth. They recognize that in order to serve God in spirit and in truth, their eyes must be on Him and not on man. They have experienced God for themselves in their own personal 25th hour experiences.

Through all the miracles, challenges and trials that have come my way, my church family's prayers, encouragement and support have sustained me and my family. Because one family decided to please and honor God by not going through with their carnal plans, I was given an honored opportunity to give my life back to Jehovah Elohim- my eternal Creator. For this, I will be eternally grateful.

Roderick and I have grown closer together through the experiences that have come into our lives. We have experienced other challenges that rocked the very foundation of our marriage, but God has proven time and time again to be faithful, loving and forgiving. Because I must learn from the Lord's example, I cannot hold on to past hurts and disappointments. My trust is in the Lord.

A loving God forgave me of all my foolishness, how then can I hold on to un-forgiveness, because someone offended me? God forbid! I am determined to live at peace will all men, to love my neighbor as myself, to pray for those who might despitefully use me and persecute me. Life is too short to live in a state of un-forgiveness. Life is too short to live in a state of selfishness or to live in a state of despair.

I thank God for every trial, every experience and I thank Him for every joy. I know that God is in every trial and that He is closer that we think. He has proven that to me.

Roderick and I are still in the making process as God grows us. Our love for each other is secure, and with each passing day we thank God for His grace and mercy extended to us. Our faith, although tested and tried has proven to be unmoved, sure- - footed and resolute. Our determination to please God is steadfast. By the grace of God and with the help of the Holy Spirit, we will fight the good fight and finish the course, all to the glory and honor of our Lord and Savior Jesus Christ.

I am honored to be in the family God divinely orchestrated for me, and I will endeavor to please the Lord with the life I live before Him and . . . them.

Appendix

Hospital Days (for more photos visit www.the25hour.biz)
(clockwise)

1. First photo. This is the photo Roderick brought to me while I was in the hospital. As you can see, he looks big! His birth weight was one pound nine ounces. In this photo, he had lost weight and was weighing one pound five ounces.

2. Struggling to live. He head was no bigger than a plum.

3. Intubated and weighing one pound. He looked like a shriveled up prune with transparent skin. All his ribs were visible.

4. My hands against his limb. My wedding ring went up his arm.

5. Roderick holding the baby the first time he was taken out of the isolette – for just a few minutes.

6/7. Rod with Mom and Dad. At this time he was struggling to breath without the respirator.

8. Peacefully asleep with wool cap and feeding tube. He was weighing about one pound twelve ounces.

Home At Last

1. First photo: A Christmas treat.

2. Rod with my mom.

3. Three generations – grandfather, father and son.

4. Photo with Rod at the door shows him with the cover over his tube.

No More Trachea Tube

1. Photo of Rod seated in chair – the day his trachea tube was removed.

2. Rod with Grandma Myrtle.

3. Rod with his baby sister- Elizabeth.

Teenage Years

1. Rod with shawl – Age of Accountability Ceremony.

2. Big brother Rod, with Elizabeth (Beth).

3. Family photo.

Beverly Caesar is available for speaking engagements and personal appearances. For more information contact Beverly at:

Bethel Gospel Tabernacle
110-25 Guy R. Brewer Blvd.
Jamaica, NY 11433

TOLL FREE: 1-888-BETHEL9 (1-888-238-4359)
EMAIL: beverlycaesar@beverlycaesar.com

To order additional copies of this book or to see a complete list of all **ADVANTAGE BOOKS™** visit our online bookstore at:

www.advantagebookstore.com

or call our toll free order number at: 1-888-383-3110

Longwood, Florida, USA

"we bring dreams to life"™
www.advbooks.com

Printed in the United States
79237LV00005B/181-498